UNIVERSITY OF CHICHESTER

# LIFE ON MARS

## THE OFFICIAL COMPANION

# LIFE | ON

# MARS

## THE OFFICIAL COMPANION

### GUY ADAMS + LEE THOMPSON

POCKET
BOOKS

New York • London • Toronto • Sydney

First Published in Great Britain by Pocket Books, 2006
An imprint of Simon and Schuster UK
A CBS Company

A CIP catalogue record for this book is available from the British Library.

1 3 5 7 9 10 8 6 4 2
ISBN-10: 1-8473-9005-6
ISBN-13: 978-1-8473-9005-9

Writer: Guy Adams
Designer: Lee Thompson
Commissioning Editor: Sally Partington

Simon & Schuster UK Ltd.
Africa House
64-78 Kingsway
London WC2B 6AH

www.simonsays.co.uk
www.kudosfilmandtv.com
www.bbc.co.uk/lifeonmars

Printed and bound in Great Britain by CPI Bath Press, Bath, United Kingdom.

# CONTENTS

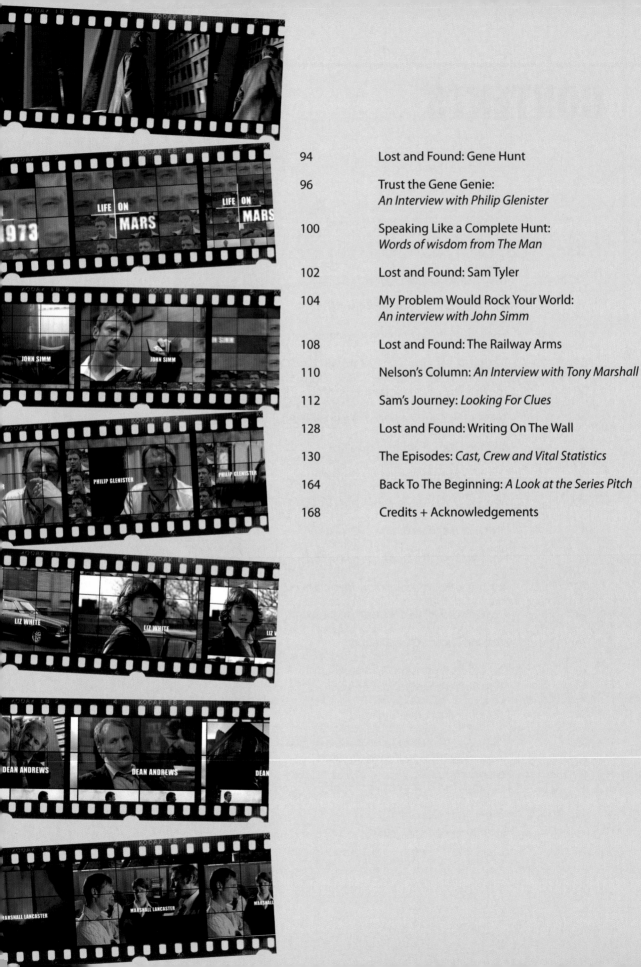

# INTRODUCTION
## MATTHEW GRAHAM

April 2005. I arrive in Manchester by train having spent the entire four-hour journey with just one song in my head, bouncing around the inside of my skull like a ping-pong ball. I catch a taxi to the BBC studios on Oxford Road. My heart is pounding. My palms are tacky. And someone inside my head turns up the volume knob on that song. I collect my BBC pass at reception and (as so often happens to writers visiting studios) become immediately lost in a rabbit warren of identical brown corridors. I finally pitch up in the rear car park. I tell myself that it's cool – I'm exactly where I want to be. I'll just mooch around the car park for a minute and then head back inside—

And then I see her.

hello gorgeous

She's sitting between a Vauxhall Astra and a Mercedes ML. Both cars are dull, nondescript colours. She is a burnished copper. There is something low-slung, wide and unapologetic about her. The minute I see her I am in love. I have dreamt of her for a long time and now she is real.

In the coming weeks I hear stories from the cast and crew about their reaction on first seeing the Cortina. Everyone wants to touch her. Sit behind her wheel. I am no different. I struggle in – the seats are devoid of anything resembling suspension. I grip her wheel gently and I whisper, 'Hello gorgeous.'

And then I catch an attendant looking at me askance and I'm out of there as if caught in an illicit tryst. I barrel through a set of double doors marked STRICTLY PRIVATE – NO ENTRY and find myself pitched up in a concrete bunker jammed with desks and clunky green phones and Page Three pin-ups and hero-photos of Georgie Best and Francis Lee nestled alongside mug-shots of killers and armed blaggers.

I am in CID, 'A' Division and I feel just like a certain Sam Tyler did the moment he burst in on the smoke-filled kingdom of one DCI Gene Hunt.

And now that insistent song that has ridden with me up from Somerset can stand it no longer and breaks out and I am singing at the top of my voice, *'Take a look at the Lawman beating up the wrong guy, Oh man! Wonder if he'll ever know, he's in the best-selling show. Is there life on Mars?'*

We're here. We've made it. Seven years after Ashley Pharoah, Tony Jordan and I thought up a bizarre, untenable idea for a TV show about a modern-day copper falling back to 1973, I am standing on the set at the start of filming for *Life On Mars*. I am marvelling at the elaborate and evocative sets, the sensationally unkempt hair and the indefatigable attention to that oh so eye-catching dress sense.

CID, 'A' Division

It's been a long journey and in these pages you'll get to read about how it started and where and why, as well as the discussions and decisions made about that hair, those clothes and that damn beautiful car. There were times during the endless development and over the course of the five-month shoot when I wondered if it was worth it. Luckily I had a seventies soundtrack at my disposal – the songs I played to inspire myself or put into the script. Some survived to broadcast. Some fell by the wayside. But they all served a purpose.

Cream's 'White Room' could always be relied upon to get me writing first thing in the morning. If I had to carry out a series of late-night script revisions then trust Deep Purple and 'Smoke On The Water' to make me revved. What better way to illustrate Sam's amazed, bewildered awe at the new world around him than The Who's opening to 'Baba O'Riley'. And as for Wings – the moment I heard that devastating guitar chorus from 'Live And Let Die' I saw sweaty, pallid, overweight men in trunks chasing one another.

Well, who wouldn't?

And at the end of every day, be it productive or disheartening (and there were plenty of both) I would play Bowie's masterpiece – melancholic, upbeat, humorous and baffling by turns. Just as I hope our drama is.

These classic tunes became the soundtrack of my life. And there were many more. You can find them all listed inside along with the other major elements of *Life On Mars* that inspired me so much. Find out why this was the only possible cast for the show. Why there is a connection between the CID set and Sam's mental state. Why the costume design is such a carefully calibrated reflection of the year. What inspirational films and TV shows the director watched before he started filming Episode One. And you may even find out why this show would not have happened without the bright lights, sandy beaches and fish and chip suppers offered up by a famous seaside resort town!

But don't just be content with writers, producers, directors and designers. Get up-close and personal with Sam, Annie, Ray and Chris and go on the search for the real Test Card Girl!

And if you're feeling up to it, how about pulling up a chair opposite the Guv himself. If you're lucky he might get the scotch out. And if you're unlucky … well let's not go there.

Whether in front or behind the camera, I thank my lucky stars for everyone involved in this production. Together these fine folk all helped to make this 'freakiest show' the weird and wonderful thing that it is.

But as Gene might say, 'That's enough nancy talk, you slag.' I'm digging out a few untapped seventies classics from my CD collection. I need inspiration to help me finish off the scripts for a little thing called Series Two …

*Matthew Graham*
*September 2006*

Me, at the porn shoot in Ep 8!

# LOST AND FOUND:
# PROLOGUE

*It's a god-awful small affair.*

But then, at the end of the right sort of day, it's the *little* things that really get to you.

'Strong coffee, lots of milk … where was the rocket science? Pretty basic request you'd have thought'

Adams stirs at the murky takeaway coffee with a plastic stirrer that seems so *perfectly* thin and flexible its inadequacy for the job in hand can only have been planned at the design stage.

Thompson looks up from his laptop, 'Buffet car badness, what do you expect?'

He looks out of the train window and watches the lights of London dash past for a few seconds.

'Yeah … ' Adams is still thrashing his drink: it's annoying him and he's taking his frustration out on it. If the Herculean mountain of Scots blue rinse digs her elbow into him *again* he'll take it out on her too, maybe even beat her senseless with the *Daily Mail* she keeps rustling and tutting over.

'I mean, seriously, I could *personally* lactate more milk than this.'

That actually makes the old woman gasp and clutch her paper in shocked fists, which makes him feel better: he might actually get some work done now.

He powers up his laptop and tries to stretch his legs under the table, working his feet – aching and hot from too many Underground tunnels and cross-city dashing – between the table leg, Thompson and the large rucksack the foreign student occupying the fourth seat has stashed there. He has a feeling she might be Russian … difficult to tell.

The screen lights up, reflecting in the thick glass of the window. He stares at the darkness outside, unsure where to begin, sipping his coffee, then wishing he hadn't as it seems to scour the enamel from his teeth as surely as rhubarb.

'What are you thinking?' Thompson asks, sweeping his wireless mouse in large flamboyant circles across the formica table.

'How to find the "in".'

Thompson looks at him. 'Hmm?'

'You know, how to get into it, how to … *immerse* myself. It needs that … to feel like an extension of the programme. Nobody wants this to be another boring "overview" style book.'

'Obviously.'

Adams sighs and starts clicking through the folders onscreen, hunting for his music files. There we go … can't beat a bit of Bowie. As a starting point to get into the mood it's as good as any, better than most; did wonders for Matthew Graham after all. He clicks it to 'play' and plugs his headphones into the side of the computer, as much to keep everyone else out as to not disturb them: he wants his head to himself.

The train pulls into a station, people disembark and Adams closes his eyes, letting himself drift.

Time passes.

It's only when the vicious *Daily Mail* reader gives him one last savage jab in the gut that he realises he's fallen asleep at some point. Trying not to look too bleary-eyed and startled, he watches her shuffle off the train and gives her a little wave through the window.

*Miss you.*

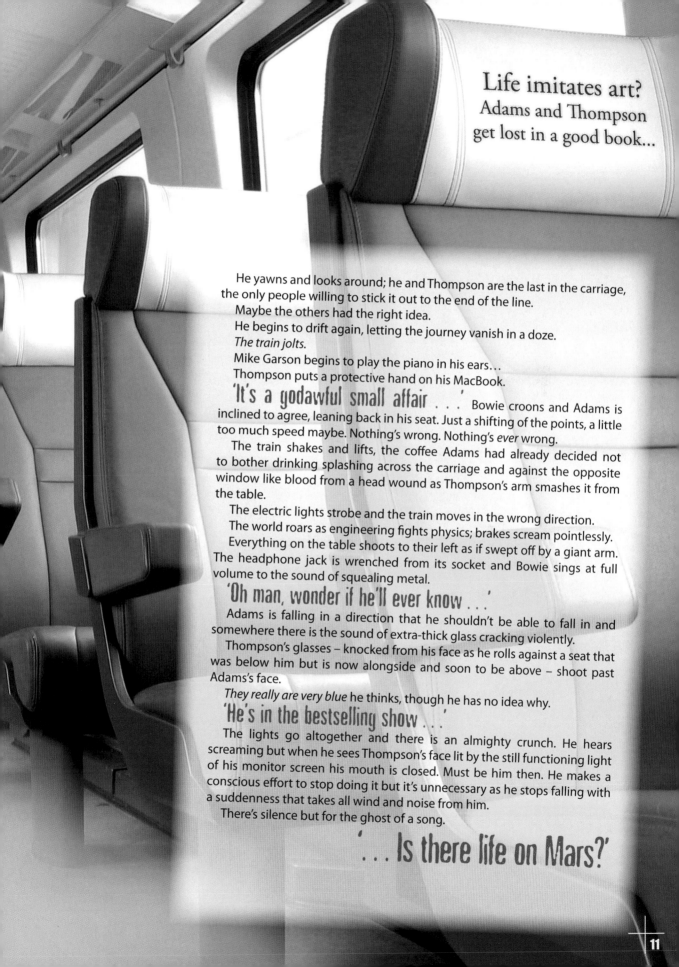

**Life imitates art?**
Adams and Thompson
get lost in a good book...

He yawns and looks around; he and Thompson are the last in the carriage, the only people willing to stick it out to the end of the line.

Maybe the others had the right idea.

He begins to drift again, letting the journey vanish in a doze.

*The train jolts.*

Mike Garson begins to play the piano in his ears…

Thompson puts a protective hand on his MacBook.

**'It's a godawful small affair . . .'** Bowie croons and Adams is inclined to agree, leaning back in his seat. Just a shifting of the points, a little too much speed maybe. Nothing's wrong. Nothing's *ever* wrong.

The train shakes and lifts, the coffee Adams had already decided not to bother drinking splashing across the carriage and against the opposite window like blood from a head wound as Thompson's arm smashes it from the table.

The electric lights strobe and the train moves in the wrong direction.

The world roars as engineering fights physics; brakes scream pointlessly.

Everything on the table shoots to their left as if swept off by a giant arm. The headphone jack is wrenched from its socket and Bowie sings at full volume to the sound of squealing metal.

**'Oh man, wonder if he'll ever know . . .'**

Adams is falling in a direction that he shouldn't be able to fall in and somewhere there is the sound of extra-thick glass cracking violently.

Thompson's glasses – knocked from his face as he rolls against a seat that was below him but is now alongside and soon to be above – shoot past Adams's face.

*They really are very blue* he thinks, though he has no idea why.

**'He's in the bestselling show . . .'**

The lights go altogether and there is an almighty crunch. He hears screaming but when he sees Thompson's face lit by the still functioning light of his monitor screen his mouth is closed. Must be him then. He makes a conscious effort to stop doing it but it's unnecessary as he stops falling with a suddenness that takes all wind and noise from him.

There's silence but for the ghost of a song.

**'. . . Is there life on Mars?'**

# THE FREAKIEST SHOW

## LIFE ON MARS

It begins normally enough, same old same old ... speeding cars, blues and twos ... just another day in cop show television. There are sharp suits, uniforms, interrogations and suspects; nothing much to differentiate it from the soup of police procedural that clogs the prime-time cathode-ray tubes. Ten minutes in, of course, and the metaphorical rug has well and truly been pulled – the lead character's been creamed by a speeding car and the audience are as awash in a sea of big collars and Paco Rabanne as DCI Sam Tyler; lost in a history so close yet so alien.

Despite the track record of Kudos Film and Television, the production company behind *Spooks* and *Hustle*, both of which were already big successes on BBC1, *Life On Mars* could so easily not have been made at all. Seven years in Development Hell – that depressing limbo inhabited by films and television shows struggling to get from the desk to the screen, where it underwent draft after draft as it bounced between broadcasting companies – could have seen it die the death of many great ideas that failed to find their audience. That it didn't is due to the effort

of, like all shows, many people. Not just Matthew Graham, Tony Jordan and Ashley Pharoah – the writers who originally came up with the concept – or Jane Featherstone and Claire Parker from Kudos who fought and challenged to get it bought and broadcast. There were design teams, costume departments, directors, editors ... not to mention the obvious work brought to the finished project by the actors chosen to bring the story to life.

It is the nature of television to appear polished, assured, *effortless* even. This is the trick of the medium, presenting us – the viewer – with easy fictions; an hour of our viewing lives that represents countless months – even years – to those who made it. Madness. No sane person would work in television.

So when it comes to pinning down how a show is made the only method is to talk to people, lots of them. It's not possible to speak to everyone. Really ... it *isn't*. (Danny Griffiths most definitely worked as an electrician on *Life On Mars* and is probably the nicest and most competent man ever to wield insulation tape, but space does not permit us to tell his story in this book...) But to flesh out the path

the show took to get to the screen, there is a list of people that can give a fair impression of that journey: the difficulties, the luck, the successes, the damned hard work. Representatives, if you will, from the various areas of production. There will always be contradictions: everybody has a different perspective within a situation; assumptions are made, conversations are only half heard or misremembered. That's life. There is no definitive history: just impressions, as accurate as possible – with a little give or take for the better repetition of a good story.

Which is as it should be.

It's all here, though, from thought (with all the changing of a mind that you could wish for) through to execution of that thought and, finally, to polished piece of television. And, frankly, that's a journey that makes Sam Tyler's seem a doddle.

Then there is another group of people without whom none of the above would have stood the slightest chance of success: the characters themselves. They may not have existed until their writers invented them; but in the medium of television – perhaps more than any other – that means little, because the people we get to know in *Life On Mars* have grown far beyond that. They've been given clothes, mannerisms, voices – they've been given *life* (cue: *mental image of a wild-haired Matthew Graham pulling the handle that will flood his rough-stitched Gene Hunt with electricity … Lightning hits … Hunt sits up, blue*

*arcs of power dancing between the splayed fingers of his string-back gloves.* 'It's alive!' *Graham shouts.*) More than that – they've developed a life of their own. They may be fictional – but they're real as hell.

**Sam Tyler:** Before his accident Sam Tyler was a graduate of modern society in his attitudes towards both policing and life in general, a man of crossed 't's and dotted 'i's to whom gut feelings were something to be avoided as surely as heartburn. Slowly, however, he seems to be changing as the world he finds himself in demands a more flexible approach. As if being thrown back in time at the very moment his

girlfriend, Maya, needed him most wasn't bad enough, Sam's experiences get even more personal as the series progresses, meeting his mother and father and realizing that his memories of his childhood have concealed a forgotten truth. He begins to hope that solving the mysteries of his past might be the answer to him finding his way home but, as series one finishes (with his father's criminality brutally exposed), he's no closer to escaping history; and the reason for his situation remains as elusive as ever.

**Gene Hunt:** Do the job, whatever it takes. Almost the exact opposite of Sam Tyler, DCI Gene Hunt follows his gut wherever it takes him. Brash, opinionated, hard-smoking and harder drinking he sees perfect law enforcement as coming from the Western school – a Clint Eastwood sheriff with a hip flask in his pocket. His contempt for Tyler's methods and attitudes are almost as strong as the distaste Sam has for his – they are not a pair of coppers one can imagine seeing eye to eye. But his respect for Sam's integrity grows over time, just as Sam learns that underneath that thuggish exterior there exists both a brain and a heart; and by the end of the first series they're even showing signs of becoming friends...

**Annie Cartwright:** A WPC in a generation that didn't really know what to do with them. A psychology graduate whose skills, brain

and intuition are rarely of use to her in a department that refuses to acknowledge they exist. A confidante – and maybe more – for Sam, her affection for him being the one thing sometimes that keeps him afloat. When Sam first arrives in 1973, Neil – Annie's 'ex' – tries to play up to Sam's belief that he's from the future, nearly driving him to suicide before admitting that he was joking. The only person who knows Sam's situation – or at least what he believes to be his situation – her urge to have him seek professional help is often counter-balanced by the feelings she has for him. From the start they seem to be drawn to each other,

route towards whatever conclusion he's set his heart on and scarcely concerned with anyone he has to shove aside on the way. Nothing would make him happier than to see Sam Tyler go under. Especially after Tyler's dogged persistence and refusal to hide the truth get Carling demoted to the rank of Detective Constable when his treatment of a suspect leads to the man's death.

**Chris Skelton:** Eager to please, with his head in the clouds, Skelton never quite knows whose side he's on – Tyler's or Hunt's. Soft? Yes. Dozy? Frequently. But perfectly capable of surprising himself – and others – by getting things right.

**Phyllis Dobbs:** The station's desk sergeant and as gentle as a rhino rolled in broken glass, Phyllis is the one woman in the station who can hold her own with the men. As hard, butch and foul-mouthed as any of the detectives on the staff, she has no patience but plenty of honour – she'll stand by her colleagues whatever happens.

**Nelson:** Bar manager at the local frequented by CID – the Railway Arms – he is something of a friend to Sam, a sympathetic ear for the young detective to bend. If the Test Card Girl represents a sort of 'spirit guide' to Sam, Nelson is her kinder flesh and blood counterpart, providing Sam with advice, guidance and, when he needs it, solace.

but circumstances get in the way and contrive to prevent them becoming more than friends. And, in spite of their feelings, issues arise which compromise the emotional trust they have.

**Ray Carling:** A man of his time, belligerent and chauvinistic, Ray has no truck with the gentle side of policing, happiest to take the quickest

# LOST AND FOUND:
# TEENAGE WASTELAND

## 'It's on Amerika's tortured brow . . .'

The music was distorted, Bowie singing inside a cake tin, fighting against the sound of city centre traffic and the tannoy announcements from the train platform behind them.

Coming to on a paint-chipped wooden bench outside a train station is not something Thompson has ever done before, being neither homeless nor sufficiently fond of alcohol to have mimicked the lifestyle of one who is.

Coming to on a bench, outside a train station *miles away from where he was last aware of being...*

## CRASH        THE SQUEAL OF METAL
## THE CRACK OF GLASS

...wearing clothes he knows for a fact he would never have bought himself – brown corduroy trousers, a tank top with all the subtle line and zigzag patterning of a television struggling for a signal and a shirt that he fears may be polyester – and surrounded by people who look to have stepped out of an old Bisto advert.

*Well, this just ups the ante of 'things that have never happened to me before' to breaking point.*

## 'Now the workers have struck for fame, 'cause Lennon's on sale again . . .'

Where is that music coming from?

Then he sees the ice-cream van to the left of the station entrance – *Manchester? What the hell am I doing in Manchester?* – and notices the chunky radio on its counter.

Adams shouts and jolts awake next to him. Possibly the startled nature of his awaking is as much to do with the brightness of the red shirt he's wearing: possibly not.

They both stare out at the length of London Road, at the sea of old cars and big hair, bright colours and muted autumn browns, trousers that are just too flared and shoes that are just too high...

Thompson looks at Adams and notices that he's holding a thick brown manila envelope in his hand.

'What...?'

Adams turns the envelope around to show him what's printed on the front: *North West District CID*

Thompson has nothing to say ...

He hasn't got any words in his head that will fit.

Because nothing fits.

Not here.

Not for at *least* another thirty years or so...

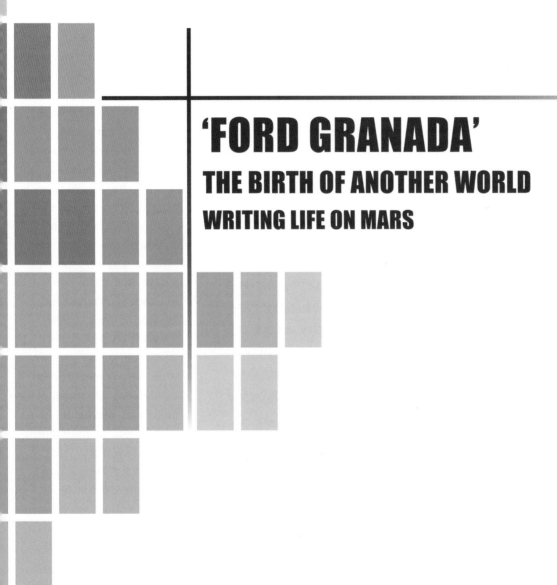

# 'FORD GRANADA'
## THE BIRTH OF ANOTHER WORLD
### WRITING LIFE ON MARS

# TONY JORDAN
## WRITER + CO-CREATOR

Blackpool?

'Well, it was my fault, really,' admits Tony Jordan. 'I was born in Southport, and Blackpool was the stomping ground of my youth. That's where all my family holidays were.

'I'd been talking to Kudos … I wanted to work with them, they wanted to work with me: the question was how we went about it. I didn't fancy the idea of being locked in an office and told to invent some show formats, so I suggested that they paid me to go away somewhere with another couple of writers, with no particular brief, and see what we all came up with. I tried to think of two writers that I really wanted to spend a weekend with, and having worked with them both on *EastEnders* I decided on Matthew and Ashley. I love collaboration with other writers; the whole always becomes greater than the sum of the parts.'

So the Blackpool jaunt was more than a weekend of Carling and candy floss on someone else's budget?

'We did it properly. We did do all the donkey rides and stuff as well – we spent hours playing on Daytona in the arcades – but we hired a small conference room and crawled in there about half past nine every morning, staying until we thought we were empty creatively and in need of another go on the videogames. It turned into a very productive weekend: I was expecting to come back with one show idea but we had five or six in the end. I suppose it helped that all three of us were used to working

that way. Matty, Ashley and I had been away before on *EastEnders* script conferences where we would be holed up for a couple of days to come up with story ideas.'

*EastEnders* and Tony Jordan are joined at the hip; it was the first show he wrote for back in 1985 and he's written over 250 episodes since. Later on he became a story consultant, liaising with the scriptwriters and producers to develop potential storylines.

So how many of the shows they came up with in Blackpool made it into production?

'We took them all to the BBC and they commissioned a pilot script for all of them bar one – the roughly titled *Island World*. Although that did later get made…by someone else entirely. It's called *Lost*. The idea was very similar but the BBC, quite rightly, felt they didn't have the budget to shoot planes crashing onto islands.'

By the time *Life On Mars* got commissioned as a series all three of them had moved on to other things, to the point where Tony was only able to write one script for the show.

'It was really difficult. If they had made the show when we first wrote it then we'd probably have done a couple of episodes each, but when it came down to it Matthew had to throw himself into it. It's his show really. He story-lined it, he wrote half the episodes… I had the horrible choice of doing *Hustle* [the other Kudos series that Tony created] or *Life On Mars*. I knew that it was safe in Matthew's hands, so I left him to it. Then of course he rings me and says, "We've got the perfect episode for you Tony, all pubs and knob gags!"'

It must be nice to have such a reputation.

> "Jane Featherstone rang me up and said 'We want to do a series about conmen and we thought of you.' I don't know why whenever someone thinks of pubs or conmen they immediately come to me…"

*Above Left to Right: Matthew Graham, Ashley Pharoah, Tony Jordan and Kudos joint managing director Stephen Garrett enjoying fish'n'chips on Blackpool seafront in 1998.*

# ASHLEY PHAROAH
## WRITER + CO-CREATOR

Second in the 1998 Blackpool Daytona Championships was Ashley Pharoah, no stranger to the creation of successful television series with *Where The Heart Is*, *Down To Earth* and *Wild at Heart* to his name. Did he take a lot of convincing to accept a weekend's jamboree at the seaside?

'What you have to remember is that Kudos weren't quite the power that they are now. The only programme of theirs I'd seen was on fishing. So when Tony asked me to join him and Matt I said, "What on earth would we want to do that for?" To which he replied, "A thousand pounds in a Waitrose bag!" We'd known each other for a long time, so the thought that I could spend a weekend with those two and a load of money was enough to get me up there. I have to say, though, that if we'd put the ideas we came up with in a list of Most Likely To Be Made, *Life On Mars* would have been at the bottom. There were a lot of strong ideas in there, and a lot of them were more conventional. Just goes to show…'

Unconventional *Life On Mars* may be, but the concept proved an immediate hit with viewers. Not to mention its writers.

'You take four very different writers – Matt, Tony, Chris [Chibnall: scriptwriter for Episode Seven] and me – and *Life On Mars* offers a format that all of them can work their way into. When we were divvying up the episodes it became clear that Tony had to write the pub one; Matt would enjoy the more 'out there' sci-fi stuff and I was drawn to the more emotional one.'

Emotional indeed, as Episode Four of the series introduces us to Sam Tyler's mother.

'I always wanted Sam to find his mum; that seemed to me to be an amazing opportunity as a writer. I felt we should reach the point where

'I've had that twice in the last few years, it was the same when Jane Featherstone at Kudos rang me up and said "We want to do a series about conmen and we thought of you." I don't know why whenever someone thinks of pubs or conmen they immediately come to me…'

Perhaps it's his witty dialogue? His sterling character work?

'I'm crap on story, I find it really hard. My stuff's always more character based; once you've found your characters, you've found your voice.'

Were the characters cast by the time he came to write his script?

'They were! I was so late with the script I was already watching rushes from the earlier episodes.'

No pressure then? Just the odd actor kicking his door down, wanting to get on with learning his lines?

'I've often thought that the way I'd like to write is the way they do Brazilian soap operas; sat in a sound booth, feeding the dialogue through the actor's earpieces: "That's right… you slap her…then walk away… Now *you* tell him he's a bastard!"'

One day, maybe.

he became slightly seduced by the era – the world – he found himself in: he's got over that "why am I here?" thing and given in to it a little. He might be in a coma; he might be dead; but if he's there he may as well enjoy himself. We certainly did! The music, the club, the dancing, the clothes… At the same time, I wanted to show that even in this world – wherever we are – actions have consequences. It's not one big game. That's why the girl, Joni, dies: she pays the price for Sam's involvement.'

As much as the format opens up plentiful opportunities for the writer, surely there are challenges too? It does possess certain limitations, after all.

'The show *is* very challenging for a writer, especially because Sam must be in every scene. That is very unusual. In television or film a lot of the tension is created by inter-cutting between the action; whereas here you're telling a story in the first person. You can't cut away the boring bits, you have to show them; just find a way to make them *interesting*. And if Sam wasn't present you can't show it at all. That's the strength but also the challenge of *Life On Mars*. It took me a few days to get into it: you have to pace yourself differently; it's an entirely different structure.

'Take the Joni character again: the conventional structure in a story like this is that you would have seen someone find her body. We can't do that. I didn't want *Sam* to find her because I wanted him to be shocked later, but we can't have *Hunt* find her and trudge upstairs to tell Sam – you just have to find other ways of doing it. I don't think for a second that an audience sits down in the pub afterwards and

> **"The show is very challenging for a writer, especially because Sam must be in every scene. That is very unusual. In television or film a lot of the tension is created by inter-cutting between the action; whereas here you're telling a story in the first person. "**

says "what an interesting first person narrative". They don't notice technically, but I think they do notice subconsciously – the *texture* of *Life On Mars* is very different.

'The other thing we realized early on is that our original police stories were too complicated. The type of story you would normally tell in that format; twists, payoffs and reveals…the concept of *Life On Mars* itself is so complex that it doesn't need complicated stories. If you look at the plots they are pretty simple. Hopefully they're *emotionally* complex, though, because they're rubbing up against Sam's condition. That was our way in to the stories: what is happening in the here and now that throws Sam's mind into the story? For me it was his mum visiting him in hospital; her voice, that's what triggers the story that follows. The crux is emotion.

'I think that's one of the reasons people like it: it is an *emotional* show. When I saw the first rough-cut of my episode I was quite moved by this stupid sock with the director's hand up it! This ridiculous glove puppet with his mum's voice should not be moving but it *is*. I love the show for that.'

# MATHEW GRAHAM
## WRITER + CO-CREATOR

Kiss-me-quick hat clamped onto unruly waves of black hair and a laugh that would challenge the automaton clown which stands at the entrance to the Pleasure Beach – albeit a little filthier – the third member of the triumvirate alongside Tony and Ashley in the queue for fish and chips was Matthew Graham.

He too has fond memories of a weekend which seems to have been as much about play as work.

'We blew about four hundred quid in one day on Daytona,' he recalls. 'We found all the ones that linked up and played it all day. At the Pleasure Beach we found they sold six-foot plastic toothbrushes so we bought a dozen of them. Then we had a mad panic when we realised that Stephen Garrett from Kudos was due to arrive that evening to see what we'd come up with. So we ran back to the hotel and scribbled all our ideas on a big white board.'

Every one a gem, no doubt.

'We came up with an invasion show called *Watford Versus Them*. It was aliens taking over an estate agents in Watford and placing other aliens in houses.

'Then there was *Water Ratz*. With a Zed. About an ex-SBS squad commander called … I forget, something awful like Tom Rock, who ran an elite, predominantly female, predominantly rubber-clad speedboat squad on the Thames. The first episode involved a bomb being placed under HMS *Belfast*. It was awful! *Island World* … Plane crash survivors on a desert island populated by ghosts. We had a telepathic rhino … ! We were taking the piss … '

There were other, less … *controversial* ideas created that weekend – and then there was some silly nonsense called *Ford Granada*.

'It was the first idea we had, realizing that, although it was the last thing *we* wanted to do, they'd probably want a cop show. So we did a straw poll of our favourite cop shows and *The Sweeney* won. From there it was just figuring out how to do it. There was no "coma" angle originally: it was just "modern-day cop falls magically back in time and ends up in *The Sweeney*." Much more basic.

'In the early drafts he wasn't sure if he'd gone back in time or whether he was mad. But the thing is, "mad" is a very nebulous concept. He's not mad; we can *see* he's not mad, he's a very sane and rational being – so it became a case of finding a scenario that could put a sane and rational being in that position.

'There was a novel called *The Bridge* by Iain Banks, which I loved, where there was this huge city built on a bridge that stretches on and on; and at the end of it the guy wakes up and we realise he's been in a coma. So I said, "let's do that, let's do a coma world!" That way he could still be the anal, obsessive, grown-up human being we wanted him to be; and yet he could

> **"At the Pleasure Beach we found they sold six-foot plastic toothbrushes so we bought a dozen of 'em! Then had a mad panic as we realised Kudos were due up that evening to see what we'd come up with."**

# GET YOUR TROUSERS ON!

Until 1975 television viewers could be mistaken for believing that there were no dangerous criminals operating in the UK. *Special Branch* had a crack at it but they were still uniformed ballerinas in comparison to the sandpaper charm and scotch-swilling stench of Inspector Jack Regan.

Originally a one-off TV Film for ITV's *Armchair Theatre* strand, *Regan* was created by Ian Kennedy Martin (brother of *Z-Cars* creator Troy Kennedy Martin) and introduced John Thaw as the first of the now rather clichéd 'maverick' detectives. The story revolved around a gangland shooting being investigated by the Flying Squad, the armed-robbery unit of the London Metropolitan Police.

The show attracted seven million viewers and was immediately commissioned as a series, the name changing to *The Sweeney* from the cockney rhyming slang term for 'Flying Squad' – Sweeney Todd.

It was phenomenally successful, turning both Thaw and Dennis Waterman as his partner George Carter into household names.

The stories tended to follow a basic structure: two acts information-gathering and witness intimidation followed by one act of tyre-squealing and head-kicking.

Audiences lapped it up.

After two series *The Sweeney* jumped to the big screen for more of the usual, albeit with fewer of the restrictions the programme makers had to adhere to for television broadcast. There then followed another two series and a movie sequel.

Finally there was a Christmas special with the rather bizarre inclusion of Morecambe and Wise – a reciprocal arrangement as both Thaw and Waterman had appeared in the comedians' Christmas Special a couple of years previously.

With a grand total of 53 TV episodes behind it *The Sweeney* left our screens but was sold to 51 countries for broadcast.

Like many 'iconic' programmes, however, it's in the legacy that it left behind that its importance can be judged in hindsight. The rebellious detective fighting against both the criminals and his superiors is now as familiar as the cop drama itself; there's no question that the gritty, hand-held, look of the show influenced countless programme makers thereafter.

constantly question his sanity, without having to act bonkers all the time. So in some ways, *Life On Mars* was inspired by Iain Banks!

'Something else I borrowed from was *The Land That Time Forgot*. In the first draft I began the episode with him finding an old box with a weird letter in it, digging up a crime scene, and then the episode ended with him burying that box. The car crash opened up a wormhole in time and space and he fell through it.'

It's clear why Ashley Pharoah pegs Matthew as the writer most comfortable with the science fiction angles, while the other members of the writing team find their inspiration in the everyday mundane, such as death and taxes. The combination made for a heady brew of proposals which they put to Stephen Garrett, Kudos's joint managing director.

According to Matthew, his reaction was brief and to the point. '"Crumbs, he said, they're going to be a hard sell. Where are we going to eat tonight?" "This is Blackpool," we told him – we took him for fish and chips and a lap dance in the end.'

But Garrett was right; the ideas the trio came up with were a very hard sell indeed. The BBC's initial response was instructive: 'They turned down *Life On Mars*, but they wanted *Water Ratz*. "That would be great for a six-thirty slot on a Saturday," they said. They paid us to go and write it. Tom would shout "Ratz, Get In 'Ere!" – a low-rent *Charlie's Angels*. It was rubbish!'

Perhaps thankfully, *Water Ratz* never saw the light of day and *Life On Mars* became Matthew's personal project, the various proposals having been

apportioned between the three of them. There were many drafts, and several alternative settings.

'The first draft was set in Brighton, the second in London; then it was *set* in London but *filmed* in Bristol, then set in Bristol and actually *filmed* in Bristol, then it was set in Leeds and then, about three weeks before we were due to start filming, it settled in Manchester.

'Once I started researching Manchester, though, I thought it would be great. The whole Mancunian Way [the large flyover alongside which Sam's accident takes place] gave us our opening – the *Back to the Future* thing, waking up and seeing the billboard announcing its forthcoming construction.'

Considering its long period of gestation – and the constant setbacks – it's amazing that *Life On Mars* ever reached our screens.

'When we first went to the BBC all those years ago it was a different team in charge and it just didn't fit their profile. So we went to Channel 4 and developed it there but, at the last minute, they balked. By that time Julie Gardner at BBC Wales was doing *Doctor Who* and we liked her and thought she might be able to convince Jane Tranter [Controller for Drama Commissioning at the BBC]. We didn't tell Julie it was a time-travelling, 1973 cop show; she just thought we were sending her a new cop show, which is what she was looking for at the time. She got ten pages in and rang us up, saying, "I'm not sure I can do another time travel show…" but she read it through to the end, and she loved it. Fair play to her, she sent it straight off to Jane Tranter – who I was convinced wouldn't go for it, but ended up commissioning it straightaway. Jane didn't worry about whether it was a genre that people were ready for. She read it and she liked it, she wasn't concerned about whether she could "sell" it, if you like.

'That spirit continued all the way through. I thought the Test Card Girl would go from the start. I never spent much time on those scenes because I *knew* they'd go – there was *no way* the BBC would allow a show to go out at primetime with a girl who comes out of the television screen and talks to the main character.' But the BBC never questioned it. On the contrary, they committed to the

*Right: Life On Mars in Brighton (top), then London (middle), then Bristol as London, then Bristol as Bristol (bottom) – the location moved around before finally settling on Manchester.*

show one hundred percent from the start. 'They even commissioned the second series the day we finished filming the first, their logic being that they didn't care if no-one else wanted to watch it, because they did!'

Does he subscribe to the suggestion that *Life On Mars* just happened to come at the right time, when both the broadcasting industry and the audience were open to its content?

'I do think that if we hit a zeitgeist, it wasn't the zeitgeist of time travel or fantasy; it was just that people were bored of the shows that they were watching. My wife's not a writer, but she'll often come up with lines that actors are about to say before they say them. At least with *Life On Mars* you couldn't predict the next line or scene.

'The big revelation for me was when I was in the States a few years ago, and *Star Trek: The Next Generation* was on at nine o'clock in the evening, not six-fifty like it was here. As far as they were concerned it was an adult drama, and I was determined to see if we could tap into that. That was what we said to Channel 4, because they were concerned that adults wouldn't watch a show like *Life On Mars*. If you go into Blockbuster, you don't see the kids getting all the sci-fi and horror while adults rent *Pride and Prejudice*. It's not like that. Go to the multiplex and look at the people who went to see *Lord of the Rings*. It isn't just children and twenty-year-olds. Those films can't make that sort of money out of one small demographic: I've never bought into the argument that sci-fi is for teens and people in their early twenties, and that once you get into your thirties and have kids of your own you immediately start

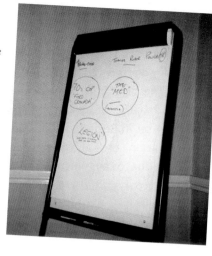

watching Richard Curtis films instead.

'Having said that, there is a level of restraint in *Life On Mars* which helps, I think. If it had been left to me I would have made it more extreme, because it's in my nature. I've grown up with different films, books and television shows from Claire Parker and Jane Featherstone [Producer and Executive Producer], which is why it works so well between us. They tell me "less is more", because they don't want the show to feel too overtly sci-fi, and I think that through pulling back a bit we've actually found the best level. It means people can watch it on one level and get all sorts of inferences, but others can watch it at a different level without feeling alienated or excluded.'

How did he feel about depicting the pragmatic and hard-nosed attitudes typified by characters like Gene Hunt and Ray Carling? Was there a concern about how they would be perceived in today's more politically correct climate? Or was the reverse the case – did he think the show might invoke a wave of nostalgia for those un-PC times when people spoke their minds without a thought for whom they were offending?

> **"There is a level of restraint in *Life On Mars* which helps, I think. If it had been left to me I would have made it more extreme, because it's in my nature."**

## "I mean who wants an overtly racist hero? It doesn't work... Although strangely the more *sexist* we made Gene the funnier he became"

'The one thing I was worried about before the show went out is that we would become fuel for the right-wing tabloid press. You know, "If Gene Hunt was in charge of immigration…" Luckily there doesn't seem to have been much of that. I never wanted him to be a poster boy for intolerance: that was why we made the decision very early on that we wouldn't embrace all the aspects of what a real Gene Hunt might have been like. I mean, who wants an overtly racist hero? It doesn't work. We tried it; it was *horrible*, nobody knew where to look. Tony Marshall, who played Nelson, was great: he would laugh and say it was fine; but it wasn't fine. Although strangely the more *sexist* we made Gene the funnier he became…

'We do tackle racism as a theme in series two. We didn't do it in series one because we didn't want people to think we were doing a show about seventies issues: this week: women, next week: wheelchairs.'

With that in mind, was there ever a doubt about how they were portraying the police force of the time?

'Steve Crimmins, our police advisor, was brilliant. When we sent him the first two episodes he rang me up and I said, "I know, it's over the top…" "No," he said, "it's not over the top enough. It's not *extreme* enough. But I can see why you have to pull back…"

Having a serving policeman advising the production team also helped them to

In this extract from the very first draft of the Life On Mars script from 1998, written by Matthew Graham, we see Sam's character being ushered through CID.

In this version, set in Brighton, the police station was Sallis Hill and Sam Tyler was called Tom Page. Kev Rodes, Raymond Pallister and DCI Hale became Chris, Ray and Gene through the various drafts that followed. Whilst the characters have changed slightly, this sequence is still very reminiscent of the final version as seen in the transmitted Episode One, including Sam's superior officer's turn of phrase…

**17. INT. SALLIS HILL. OFFICE. DAY.**

TOM sits alone sipping tea. Notices his hand trembling, rattling the tea cup. Clenches his fist against it. The office is naturally decked out in the style of the times. TOM cannot believe the clunky black telephone on the desk.

Two men enter. The first is DC KEV RODES. KEV is mid 20s. Lithe. Sexy. Black polo neck under a black leather jacket. He wouldn't look out of place in a 90s club like Starsky And Hutch. The second is DCI RAYMOND PALLISTER. 40s. Clean-cut. No bullshit. Conservative grey suit.

**18. INT. SALLIS HILL. CORRIDOR/CID. DAY.**

KEV leads TOM through the drab corridor towards CID. He talks ten to the dozen with a big cheerful grin on his face... They emerge into an open-plan room that is literally soupy with fag smoke. TOM balks. Coughs. Five pairs of eyes turn to him. DCs and DS. All men. Four smoking.

**TOM:** Uhh... is the air-con busted sir?

**KEV:** Air-con?!

**HALE:** Yeah the air-con's busted and our Tardis is in the garage for repairs so you find us muddling along a bit at the moment. Billy open a window.

TOM is out of his depth here but his character is such that he is prepared to sit tight for now and see what develops.

GENE

CAR SPEEDS THRU' ST
NEWSPAPERS FLY.

**Above:** *Brian Sykes' storyboard illustrations for a scene from Episode Three showing the Cortina whizzing overhead. This sketch is one of the favourites amongst the production crew, and even adorns the production office walls as a piece of art.*
**This page, top left to bottom right:** *Brian Sykes' storyboards showing the proposed crash sequence, which was originally planned to take place on the Mancunian Way and finish with a special effects shot zooming in on Sam's eye to show stars and galaxies.*

understand the pressures of police work, brought home in occasional moments of real-life drama. 'I called him once,' Matthew remembers. '"Hi, Steve," I said, "I was just twiddling my thumbs thinking about this idea and I thought I'd run it past you." He said, "It's a bad time at the moment, Matthew, a girl's just been murdered." I didn't know what to say…'

Was there anything in the making of the show which, given the opportunity, he would like to have done differently?

'I wish we could have afforded to put more cars on the road. Whenever there's a car chase the roads are suspiciously empty; the same four cars parked at intervals… And I'd love to have had more scenes like the record shop in Episode One where Sam says, "look" and 'Baba O'Riley' by The Who starts playing. Originally, in the script, we're looking down the streets and seeing all the iconic seventies shops we could think of. But it isn't possible to do expensive GCI shots like that all the time. Producers always say, "Don't think about the budget, allow your mind to create." Then they get the script and say, "a Pterodactyl! Riding other Pterodactyls! What were you thinking, Matthew!?"

Between page and screen the writer also has to hand his creation over to the actors to interpret. What was it like for him watching his central character of Sam Tyler brought to life by the talent of John Simm?

'John is the most instinctive actor I've ever met, he's just amazing. He reads the line in one go and he's got it. His awareness of camera and what's going on about him is phenomenal. I always said to him that he'd got the Tom Cruise role in *Rain* *Man*: his job was to make what Phil does make sense. He's the one that grounds those two characters. That's why the characters work so well together: without Sam, Gene doesn't make sense; and without Gene, Sam alone wouldn't be interesting enough. They compliment one another perfectly.'

Matthew is also endearingly honest about the creative process: the almost organic way in which the parts produce the whole.

'We didn't make this thing knowing exactly how we should do it: we kind of fumbled our way into it, going back over ourselves and patching things up. A lot of *Life On Mars* is about filming an episode and asking each other whether it works. "Should we shoot another bit of this or do an extra bit for that?" A lot of the threads in series one for example – those little page-boy shoes running through the woods – were put in at very last minute. It was in our heads from the start that we were going to do something like that but we didn't actually do it until much later.

> ## "Without Sam, Gene doesn't make sense; without Gene, Sam just wouldn't be interesting enough! They compliment one another perfectly"

'People think that everything is planned from the beginning, but creativity doesn't work that way. It's messy. Every time I have to write a new episode, I'm scared: I sit at my desk, head in my hands, and wonder what the hell I'm going to do. That's why I don't go on the forums any more, because I don't want to know that there are all these people waiting to know what I'm writing. I love 'em to bits, and god bless them for supporting the show, but I don't want to hear their expectations.

'I have to keep saying to myself, "Don't worry, Matt, it's your show. Just do what you do and they'll be fine."'

# CHRIS CHIBNALL
## WRITER

Chris Chibnall is the only writer to have worked on the first series who wasn't involved at its creation, the only man lucky enough to swoop in and play with the other writers' toys for an hour.

'I was working with Kudos on another project, and Claire Parker rang me up and told me they had one slot free on *Life On Mars* and they'd like me to do it. She sent me the first script and I was so blown away by it that I decided I had to do it; it had everything you could wish for, and it was so *clear*. You later discover that Matthew had spent thirty-four drafts getting it to that point – but it *was* so fantastically clear, and it had a great sense of fun and well-defined characters. If you're a guest writer on a show, what you're looking for is great characters in an interesting world, so to have that from the off made it an easy job to say yes to.'

Ashley Pharoah has commented on the show's accessibility for different writers; that there's something there for everyone to play with, and Chris agrees.

'There's an iconography to the characters that's part of its strength; there's fantasy and time travel and questions over the coma; but, at its heart, it's a buddy movie, and who doesn't want to write a buddy movie?

'And the dynamic makes such sense. It's a simple dynamic between Sam and Gene on the one hand but it's also incredibly complicated on the other, because it's not that Sam is always right, and it's not that Gene is always right; they both learn things from each other, they're *both* wrong. So it's emotionally complex, comically complex and narratively complex; from a simple starting point, it gets very messy very quickly, which gives you so much scope.

'I read Ashley's Episode Four, which just made me cry as soon as I read it, and then Tony's

> ## "It's emotionally complex, comically complex and narratively complex; from a simple starting point, it gets very messy very quickly, which gives you so much scope"

episode set in the pub had so much energy and brio and fun – you could see that there was incredible potential.

'I didn't have a clue what I was going to do with my episode [Seven] until I sat in on the script reading for Episode Five, and Tony was talking about Ray. He was asking, "Who is he, and what motivates him?" – so it started from there really.'

And got darker from there on.

'Yes, I would say it's the darkest of the first series; and it also became a lot more integral to the flow of the show as a whole than I expected… We never consciously talked about the 'arc' of the series in terms of story-lining that episode – it was very much going to be a standalone thing – but through various drafts and watching as the series direction became clearer, it kind of slotted together more. It certainly wasn't rigorously planned from the start; the web of it all, Sam destroying his world with the cassette as well as the death in custody plot. It came very late on, third or fourth draft, I think, from Jane Featherstone, who saw the connection between the two stories. So it may look beautifully smoothed in to the overall flow of the series, but at the beginning it was very much standalone.

'Up until that point nothing had really cost a huge amount in terms of drama and emotion. There had been lots of emotional plot but little in the way of direct consequence. The very first conversation I had was 'death in custody', which I kind of leapt on, thinking there was no way they would let me do it but everybody – Claire, Jane, Matthew – just said "Go as far as you want with it, we can always pull you back." They never did. I was very lucky because Matt, Ash and Tony had done all the hard work, making the audience love the characters. I then get to come in, make things darker and dig a bit.

'It's such a brilliant slot, Episodes Seven and Eight, because people are gearing up for the series finale; there's no way I could have told that story in Episode Three. It was always going to be a character piece: I watched the Roger Graef documentary *Police* – which was first screened back in 1981 – and there was an episode in that called "Death in Custody". I was horrified to see how they covered it up, and I just drew on that and applied it to our characters.

'You had to be careful not to go too far. Before we started filming we said, "let's kill Ray off." Then of course Dean comes in and he's so fantastic and integral to the show that we couldn't go down that route. Matthew described it the best way: just after the first read through – which was *very* dark – he said, "You have to bring it back at the end; it's not the end of the world, it's just that a bad man has been left in charge of the Enterprise bridge!"'

**TX SCRIPT EXTRACT - Episode Seven**

**INT. POLICE STATION/CORRIDOR - DAY 7/3**
*SAM stops outside RATHBONE's office, takes a deep breath. He walks down the corridor as if in a trance. GENE is leaning against the other corridor wall, arms folded. He heard it all.*
**GENE:** He didn't do anything, did he?
*SAM stops, turns to GENE.*
**GENE:** Way of the world.
**SAM:** A world which creates coppers like Ray. Awash with institutionalised corruption. You know, people like Rathbone need to be surgically removed from the force.
**GENE:** We can't change this world, Sam. Only learn how to survive in it.
**SAM:** I don't give up that easily.
**GENE:** Good.
*A moment between them. Then GENE walks off leaving SAM alone in the corridor.*
*As SAM carries on we see ANNIE in the other room, she watches him walk past.*

CUT TO:

**INT. POLICE STATION - DAY 7/3**
*SAM enters the room where ANNIE is, he looks surprised to see her there. He walks over to her, apologetic.*
**SAM:** I had to do it.
**ANNIE:** So I do mean that little to you?
*SAM shakes his head.*
**SAM:** You're the only one who understands.
**ANNIE:** But you could have destroyed me. All of us.
*He turns away from her. Sighs heavily.*
**SAM:** Why am I still here? Nothing I do makes any difference.
**ANNIE:** Is that what you really think?
*ANNIE turns to walk away. SAM tries to stop her, begging. She stops in her tracks.*
**SAM:** Don't abandon me, Annie. Please.

# TESTING, TESTING

*'Do you not like me with my clown?*
*I can see I make you frown.*
*When on earth will all this end?*
*I'm your friend, your only friend.'*

Test Card Girl dialogue, Episode Two

With her fixed smile and her eerie, enigmatic messages, the Test Card Girl has become an iconic image of *Life On Mars*, a signature of the show's unsettling edge. Is she really some kind of vehicle for clues to Sam's predicament, or is she merely a figment of his fevered imagination? It's amazing that a small girl playing noughts and crosses can inject such an air of genuine menace into a television drama – but how many fans of her cryptic couplets know the story of the real Test Card Girl...?

If asked for the longest running piece of television in history, the one broadcast that has clocked up more airtime than anything else, one could reasonably expect many answers. There would be talk of *Coronation Street* of course... it's a sure-fire pub-quiz response: quite wrong, but it would no doubt net you a coffee-maker on *Family Fortunes*. The fact is that one girl and her clown thrash it by a long chalk. Test Card F has logged a rough total of 70,000 hours during its thirty-plus years of transmission.

Designed as a practical method for engineers to identify tuning problems when installing televisions, the seemingly innocuous scene is actually a mass of information for testing the synchronisation, saturation, linearity and convergence of a broadcast signal. Test cards have been in use since just after the Second World War, initially as physical images held up by a member of the studio staff for the camera operator to calibrate and focus on, then a slide image and, later still, a digital transmission.

The birth of colour television in 1967 meant that the previous arrays of greyscale lines and patterns needed to be replaced with something far more ... well ... *colourful*. Most particularly the card would need to have a person on it in order to check flesh tones. BBC Engineer George Hersee took up the task. Using his two daughters Carole and Gillian as photographic place markers he drafted a card to cover all of the necessary calibrations and presented it to his employers. Discussions were had as to who or what the portrait would be, the main concern being how quickly the image might appear dated – and therefore need replacing – owing to shifting fashions and hairstyles. The use of a child seemed a perfect solution and George was asked to bring Carole, his eldest, in for a professional photo session.

The shoot was meticulously planned: the image needed to include precise shades of red, blue, green and yellow in order to function as intended. The clown – Bubbles by name – was Carole's own, although his green body was a replacement cover for the blue and white stripes he had originally sported. His buttons are also a visual aid: colour televisions separate the red, green and blue signals from the black and white ones, translating them individually. The colours take longer, so your telly holds back

the black and white signals so that they can be synchronised. Should this go wrong – a 'Chrominance Delay' issue no less – then the yellow of the clown's buttons will shift to the right, leaving the buttons plain white.

The noughts and crosses board provides another practical use, the chalk cross marking the centre of the screen.

Carole was paid £100 for the job – a fair sum of money in those days – and thought little of it … until the fan mail came in. Press attention followed every now and then and, in 1971, she was honoured at the Pye Television Awards for her role in helping to sell colour televisions. The experience didn't, as might be expected, make her hanker for further televisual exposure and – as her handmade clown attests – a skill in needlecraft led her instead to a career in theatrical costuming. There was an attempt to get her listed in the Guinness Book of Records but as her marathon screen-time couldn't be beaten – the rules state that all records must be open to challenge – she was ineligible for entry.

Test Card F was adapted in 1999 to create a variation known as J – the central cross was repositioned slightly along with other minor adjustments – and a widescreen version christened, cleverly, W.

In these days of twenty-four-hour

*Above Left: The Original Test Card F.*

*Above: Rafaella Hutchinson takes over the mantle of 'Test Card Girl' complete with replica Bubbles the clown.*

*Below: The eerily empty test card also used*

programming and automatic tuning it could be argued that the test card has had its day. It's certainly no longer the staple viewing that it once was. 'The BBC is in the business of broadcasting programmes, not the test card,' according to one engineer. Now that BBC1 runs *BBC News 24* through the early hours and BBC2 does the same with *The Learning Zone* a test card is a rare sight on our screens, generally appearing only when *The Learning Zone* is absent. If it were to vanish altogether, many would neither notice nor mourn its passing; yet Carole and her clown will always hold a distinguished place in television history.

Today fans of the test card (and in particular the music that was often played to accompany it) need look no further than The Test Card Circle, a society of over 200 enthusiasts who produce a quarterly magazine on the subject and hold annual conventions.

Go on, you know want to… Google 'em.

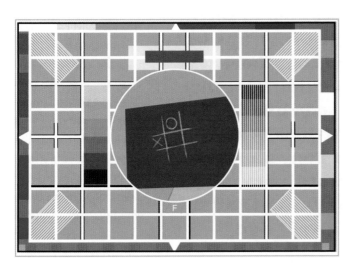

# THE PRODUCERS

## Claire Parker – Producer
## Jane Featherstone – Executive Producer

The job of television producer is, unquestionably, as vital as it is completely beyond the understanding of a good majority of viewers. Most wouldn't look that deeply into the mechanics of the show they've just watched but if they did, it's certain that a good many would have no idea what role the producer actually fulfils.

'I'm not even sure my mum knows what I do!' Claire Parker laughs, 'Every producer is different, but basically you're the one person who is across every single element of the production, not just from the development – because I worked on the series for two years before we even got the green light to make it – but throughout the whole process, from the smallest decisions to the biggest. You're the focal point, I suppose. To be confident of the vision for the show and to keep hold of that, come what may. I make sure I appoint the best people and that everyone is working to the same brief, but also hopefully empower them to push, challenge, and enrich the show at every level. From hiring the writers and directors to choosing Gene Hunt's shoes – its quite a wide remit!'

And the executive producer?

'Takes that to the next level,' says Jane Featherstone. 'Through Kudos and the broadcasters, I read every script, I see all the rushes, I check every cut; I'm involved with the casting, the budget...'

In order to get a particular 'vision' on screen, from a story in a writer's head to eight hours of acted, filmed, lit, designed, edited, costumed, sound-tracked and broadcast television it takes one hell of a lot of work, organisation and – especially with a show that had as long a gestation as *Life On Mars* – dedication, commitment and faith.

'I don't know if the show appears effortless,' says Jane. 'It probably doesn't, although I don't think the pictures quite tell the pain, heartache and work that Matthew, Claire and everybody put into it over the years. But that's fine; you don't want it to, it shouldn't show: it's bad if it starts to show.

'It was a dead project for a number of years after the BBC had originally rejected it. Then Channel 4 were looking for new projects and out it came from the bottom of the drawer – in a very different form at that time: no coma element, not really a buddy show as such, it was much more mainstream, a bit more eight o'clock in its tone really! I sat down with Matthew and Claire and we looked to see how we could reinvent it to make it something that would better suit the channel. Matthew came up with the idea of playing with whether Sam was in a coma and we worked progressively from there,

> "There were times when I think we all just wanted to throw in the towel; but we knew that there was something here that was so brilliant: that Matthew, Ashley and Tony had such extraordinary minds that we just had to give it a go."

adding the buddy cop element, Sam being a man from then and now; all added over about thirty drafts.

'We developed it for about two-and-a-half years with John Yorke at Channel 4. I kept ringing Matthew, saying "I've got some more notes and changes", and there were times when I think we all just wanted to throw in the towel; but we knew that there was something here that was so brilliant: that he, Ashley Pharoah and Tony Jordan had such extraordinary minds that we just had to give it a go. *Spooks* took hundreds of drafts before getting on screen so I was used to working that

process. We just kept pushing and pushing, then eventually Channel 4 said no!'

'That was a real low point,' Claire adds. 'I was head of development at Kudos at the time and I was working across maybe twenty similar projects, but some shows get under your skin, and this was one of them: it felt awful when it was rejected. I did think the project was dead.'

Still Kudos refused to give up. 'I went in to talk to the various people there,' Jane continues, 'and they said, "We think it's a bit silly and we're not sure how you'll make it." I sat down, *told* them how we'd make it and they still didn't go for it. So, after all this time of believing it was going to be a green light at any point, it didn't happen.

'I'd just been out to lunch with Julie Gardner, who was Head of Drama at BBC Wales, and I rang her up and asked her if she'd read it. Within twenty-four hours she came back to me saying "I love it!" in her wonderful Welsh voice. She took it to Jane Tranter – Controller for Drama Commissioning – who happened to have a gap in her schedule: it was sort of serendipity in a way, as these things

**Above:** *Jane Featherstone, Executive Producer for* Life On Mars, Spooks *and* Hustle *is also* Joint Managing Director of Kudos.
**Top Right:** *Producer Claire Parker, who worked as Kudos' Head of Development for many years.* Life On Mars *was one of the many titles she helped develop.*

often are. We went in for a meeting three or four days later, there was a green light and could we start immediately! We'd got lucky, as it turned out.'

Claire takes up the story 'We set about casting it: John Simm read the script within twenty-four hours and we offered it to him straight away. We'd always wanted Bharat Nalluri to direct, so he was on board very quickly. It was amazing – after seven years development in total it got agreed in a matter of days; it was quite a remarkable turning point. It was right that it ended up with BBC1 and not Channel 4 I think: with the BBC it was a ground-breaking, risk-taking show, noticed by seven million people.'

It became a main-stream drama rather than a cult show.

Claire agrees. 'I felt very strongly that *Life on Mars* was first and foremost a human drama – about one man's journey to find the truth about what has happened to him. But we were aware that its high concept might initially put commissioners off. We thought at script stage it might be regarded

as a niche drama; perhaps more suited to Channel 4, which has generally been less mainstream, prepared to go out on a limb. But when we sent it to the BBC we didn't change the concept at all between channels. And it really struck a chord at the BBC.'

'*Life On Mars*,' Jane explains, 'is so unique, original and interesting but, because we'd developed it for so long, we were comfortable with the 'high concept' nature of it. It didn't seem bizarre at all to me, and after the BBC said they didn't think it was bizarre either we just got on with it. I think the execution was critical to the success of the show. Bharat did a terrific visualization for the piece and Claire did a brilliant job of producing so that script, concept and the visual stuff all met in the middle. We could have tripped up a hundred times and found the standard dropping along the way.'

'I was amazed at how much the idea, the possibilities and the originality of the concept really excited everyone at every stage,' Claire adds. 'From the script through to the finishing touches in sound and picture post-production a year later, everyone was so enthused that there were constant suggestions and layers which we kept building on all the way through. Lots of the coma stuff, for example, was added later. It was wonderful that all our ambitions were fulfilled and that everyone who joined the process along the way not only

> **"From the script through to the finishing touches in sound and picture post-production a year later, everyone was so enthused that there were constant suggestions and layers which we kept building on all the way through."**

*Above: Cast and crew gather around the Cortina at the end of filming Episode Eight. Jane and Claire are standing fourth and fifth in from the right.*

gelled, but also fed off each other. That's the best position to be in really: when someone doesn't just do what you hoped for but actually surprises you and does even more. I look at the end product and, while of course there are elements that I wish we could do again, I am so proud of what we achieved.'

2006 marked something of a sea-change in the attitudes of series commissioners, as shows like *Life On Mars* or *Doctor Who* proved that, when done well, there is a huge aud-ience for programmes outside the mainstream, something Jane is determined to build on.

'I think the lesson I've learned for making other drama series is to trust the audience to be clever enough to *get* stuff. They have an extraordinary capacity to be adaptable, to interpret good story-telling, and they love being challenged – we all do. With *Life On Mars* you've got the building blocks of a traditional cop show – there

> **"I think the lesson I've learned for making other drama series is to trust the audience to be clever enough to *get* stuff, to interpret good story-telling, and they love being challenged – we all do."**

is that familiar route in for the audience – but from there we can go much further, tell many different stories. You have to keep pushing the ideas, and I think the length of the development period on this show was its greatest asset – it allowed us to add a layer each time and make it more interesting. The first draft wasn't layered: it was a similar concept, but it was much more simplistic, whereas now what you have is a traditional cop show, a buddy show, a fish out of water, a manin-a-coma-or-is-he-mad and a love story; and because of that you have something that potentially appeals to so many people.'

The trick is in finding that 'soup of a show' without it becoming horribly messy.

'Definitely, and I think that comes from its years of development. I shouldn't be advocating it but I think some shows need it; some things are *complex,* they need thinking and rethinking and that is a lesson for the future.'

# BEHIND THE CAMERA
## Bharat Nalluri – Director, Episodes 1 + 2

The strong visual style is one of the most distinctive elements of *Life On Mars*. And it took a top team of directors to create it - Bharat Nalluri, John McKay, SJ Clarkson and John Alexander. But with *Spooks* and *Hustle* already under his belt, there was only one man Kudos wanted on board to set the pace for those crucial opening episodes: Bharat Nalluri.

Having directed the British thriller *Downtime* – the story of a Newcastle tower block under siege by a bunch of thugs – Bharat spent a number of years in America working as a second unit director with Paul Anderson on both *Resident Evil* and *Aliens Vs Predator* and helming *The Crow: Salvation*, the third in the horror franchise.

'Having done the Hollywood bit for a while I thought I'd come back and do really gritty, handheld, dirty, low-fi telly, something a bit different. Everybody else had been thinking the same thing, though, as television was full of it. Directors like Paul Greengrass – who has subsequently transferred that style back to the cinema with films like *The Bourne Supremacy* and *United 93*. So I thought, okay, lets go back to the cinematic roots then… let's make things slick and glossy – sexy cinematic telly. *Spooks* has that feel and *Hustle* was probably the pinnacle, where we really pushed the boat out. It's not surprising that those shows are doing really well back in America, they understand the cinematic feel of them over there.'

The cinematic nature of Bharat's work is often discussed in reviews of the shows – that sense of bringing a big-screen atmosphere to a small-screen programme – but he doesn't believe his directing style is solely rooted in the movie ethos.

'I love the cinema but I would say that my style was influenced just as much by television of the late sixties and seventies, which was so entertainment based: *Man from U.N.C.L.E*, *Man in a Suitcase*, *The Champions* – I mean, *The Champions*, how ridiculously brilliant is that? High concept drama! [High concept indeed, it concerns three United Nations Intelligence agents who, after a plane crash in the Himalayas, are given super powers by the advanced civilization that rescues them.] It was really that which I pitched for when I first started working with Kudos. The twist we add to that high concept now is to try and make it believable, which is why those sorts of shows are working again. You can't just rely on the concepts any more. The new *Doctor Who* is a great example of how to get it right – put some *real* people in it and you care, you know?

'Genre television is very hard to do. It's difficult to suspend an audience's disbelief and get them to invest in the characters. A naturalistic drama is easy in those terms because the world is instantly recognisable as "real". But when you bend that reality … well, that's the job, getting people to believe it. Genre TV does open up an Aladdin's cave of options in terms of

> **"Genre TV is very hard to do, it's difficult to get that believability to the story; to suspend an audience's disbelief and get them to invest in the characters. "**

drama but the trick is to hone it and keep it controlled, so it doesn't just become fantasy for fantasy sake. It's got to revolve around your central character; it's got to have real dramatic intent.'

Was Bharat concerned with the viability of 'selling' *Life On Mars* to an audience?

'Of course, it's a really fine line between cocking up and creating something new and innovative. You've just got to put your stall out and do your best. There's always that danger: even when we were making it, we wondered whether anyone would get it because it was so 'out there'. But, when I first got the script I thought, "We have to make this, it's so amazing!" so I hoped that others would get the same thing from seeing it as I did from reading it.'

As if the idea of a time-travelling cop wasn't tough enough, the show came with another built-in hurdle: the need to recreate the era in which it was set without descending into nostalgia or cliché.

'That was the key for me, and my first involvement, really. I didn't want it to be this nice, nostalgic trip to 1973 full of glam rock and backlit in this hazy sunshine that everyone seems to remember. So I thought back to where I'm from, which was Newcastle. The seventies I remember in Newcastle were hard and difficult. Fun, because I was a kid, but a really hard time nonetheless – the coal strike, the power disputes, it was pretty nasty – and I didn't want people to get into it and just reminisce.

'I went back to the movies that were made at the time, to tap into that mood. *Get Carter* was good because it was from 1972. It's a very hard piece, very visceral, and the only people who had money, status, "bling" were the villains. Everybody else had *one* suit, that was it, and

**Above Top:** *Director Bharat Nalluri, Producer Claire Parker and John Simm enjoy a moment off-camera during the filming of Episode One.*

**Above Middle:** *The original cast of MI5 agents in the award-winning BBC drama* **Spooks***, another of the Nalluri-directed programmes produced by Kudos Film and Television.*

**Above Bottom:** *The grifters of* Hustle, *the Kudos-produced BBC drama from an idea by Bharat, also with his direction.*

they wore that to the office or to funerals!'

Although, it has to be said, *Life On Mars* doesn't match *Get Carter* for grimness. It would have been a pretty depressing series if it had. And rough as DCI Gene Hunt is, he's a pillar of rectitude next to Michael Caine's vengeful gangster Jack Carter.

'That's the thing, if you look at the character of Gene Hunt, he could be perceived as quite a nasty bloke, so you have to create that "heart of gold" element. Gene is someone who is going to do the right thing in the end; intrinsically he's a good man. One inspiration for me was Orson Welles in *A Touch of Evil*. Welles plays Hank Quinlan, this huge, crooked police captain who arrests and charges suspects without evidence. But the point is, most of the time he's *right*; the people he pursues are guilty. His instinct is very strong: that's the framework I saw Gene in.'

When it came to casting a leading man capable of carrying off the fantastical premise – not to mention holding his own next to Phil Glenister's Hunt – how did Bharat go about finding the right man for the job?

'What I've always looked for is someone who can deliver the truth. Once you've done that my job is easy: if an audience believes your leading man you're onto a winner. We've a history at Kudos of slightly unpredictable casting. When we did *Spooks* some people doubted that Matthew McFadyen was the right person; that he was ideal was proven as soon as the show first aired. With *Hustle* we took Adrian Lester, this hugely respected Royal Shakespeare Company actor, and put him in the heart of that set-up. And then with John Simm we went for the best actor who could deliver that particular story. It's

> **"What I've always looked for is someone who can deliver the truth. Once you've done that my job is easy: if an audience believes your leading man you're onto a winner."**

through Sam's eyes that we see it all so the actor playing him is pivotal. John's from that world – the North West – and I knew he could deliver the idea; he got it straight away. It wasn't the overtly heroic characterisation that some would have made it but he gives you so many options: he's the one who opened the show up for further series in my opinion. It could have been a one-note performance from some people.'

As well as the casting, Bharat was determined to create the right atmosphere for the show, working closely with the costume and design teams to bring the image of the seventies he wanted onto the screen.

'There was a very specific look that Adam Suschitzky, Director of Photography, and I pushed for in the series. *Life On Mars* was a very hard show to get across to television executives. It's a very *brown* show; the colours I remember from my youth, brown, burnt umber, maroon… which is what I wanted to get across; but most television people have been brought up with the view that bright telly is good telly. It was only because of the success of *Spooks* and *Hustle* that the BBC let us get on with it, I think.

'We also experimented with lens flares: pointing the cameras at lights and getting these organic flares, which is a real no-no these days, but a very seventies thing to do. You go back to films like *The French Connection* and they're full of all that – people don't consciously recognise it but *subliminally* it feels real and of its time. The costume was also very carefully done, so that it didn't play up against the background. That's the other thing that often happens when people do a seventies piece. You get very over-the-top

backgrounds and foregrounds, so you don't know where to look: it's like a paint explosion. My job is to make you look at the actor.'

When it finally came to shooting the first episode of the show the finished cut overran considerably – clocking in at nearly eighty minutes.

'It was a bit long but it's an in-house style we developed on *Spooks*. Normally you have a sixty page script for sixty minutes of television but with *Spooks* we had a *seventy-five* page script. There was a lot of talk as to whether we should cut it down but in the end I insisted we film it all because we then take seventy-five minutes and cram it into sixty minutes. It's a *West Wing* trick actually, they cram a lot of dialogue into the show and that gives it pace. The pacing of Kudos productions has more of a pulse than a lot of dramas precisely because we overshoot and then condense it down. Originally we had a big slice of Sam's present-day

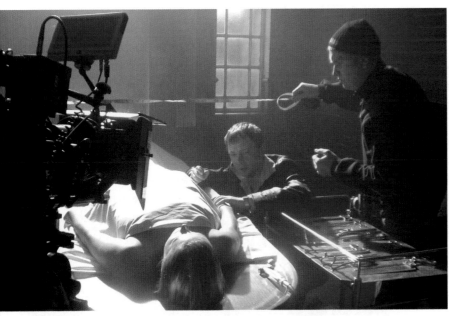

*Right, Top to Bottom: Sam Tyler from 2006 to 1973. **Above:** Camera crews line up the shot where Sam discovers the fibres under the victim's giner nails in Episode One.*

life; we were with him for maybe ten minutes more – but I felt we didn't need it, the story kick-starts when he gets hit by the car, so I just cut it and we learn about his life in the future by how he interacts with the past.'

With so heavy an involvement in the visual creation of the show it must have been hard for Bharat to walk away, his job done, after the first two episodes.

'In some ways, I felt very protective of *Life On Mars*, in the sense that I wanted it to succeed. I also wanted to leave a strong template for others to follow and for the actors to work in. But it's important that other people can come in and expand it, particularly if a show goes to a second series; you need that new influx of people. It is difficult though. If I could have directed every episode, I would have done.'

# FEEL THE FORCE
## A Police Perspective

It's important with a show like *Life On Mars* – a show that begs the question 'was it really like that?' almost weekly – that you have reliable research and some expert advice on hand to confirm the finer details of seventies policing. Having a man like Steve Crimmins on the end of the phone as a police advisor is, therefore, invaluable. A serving police officer based in the north west of England with the rank of Detective Inspector, he worked on the force back in 1973 and knows *exactly* what a typical northern CID office was like.

'There were a few broadminded people in CID,' he acknowledges, 'but Gene and Ray are fairly representative. Ultimately, no matter how many intellectual or liberal-minded officers there were, the hard core of people would have been like Ray, and usually they were extremely influential. They were powerful, no-nonsense characters, and, I have to say, they knew what they were doing.

So was the force in those days really peopled by outsize personalities like *The Sweeney*'s Jack Regan or our own Gene Hunt, or are such fictional giants written larger than life for dramatic effect?

Steve gives the nod to their veracity. 'People worked the force with personality, then, more than regulation. To be a successful DCI you really did have to be a bit like Gene Hunt: you had to be able to control your men, they had to be frightened of you.'

And does he think a return to that style of policing, those personalities within the force, would be a good thing?

'No…' His reply is emphatic. 'People like that would be no use today, they would create so many problems for themselves that nobody would want to work with them: they'd be shunned, and rightly so. There is an element to those days that appeals to an audience, though. If you look at Sam and Gene, in many ways, the personal commitment that Gene shows – which would have been fairly common then – is far *more* than Sam's; because Sam works by the rules all the time, which means that whether you catch the guy or not, you're never going to get in any trouble. Gene puts his neck on the line, Sam doesn't; and I think that's what people like about it. As the expression goes, you want someone who can *get the job done* – and Gene does.

'Mind you, it really was a different time… you must remember that back then, *all* crime was dealt with by detectives: even five pounds' worth of criminal damage was a Chief Inspector's job! Also it was all about "detections" – the statistical points you would earn for each case solved. We're moving towards that sort of thing now, but it was the be-all and end-all back then. Detectives who couldn't get enough detections would end up in ridiculous situations, involved with trivial things way beneath their training, all because they were trying to increase their detection rate.

> **"You must remember that back then, all crime was dealt with by detectives: even five pounds' worth of criminal damage was a Chief Inspector's job!"**

'Years ago,' he remembers, 'I was working in Lancashire when we had a spate of garden gnomes being nicked; which is mildly annoying if you happen to like garden gnomes, but it's not exactly the crime of the century, is it? We had about two dozen reported; they were going missing left, right and centre. One night there was a police constable out on patrol and he saw a lad with a gnome under his arm, who threw it away and ran when he was challenged. The PC caught him and next morning, when the detectives came on duty, one of them took over the job. He searched the lad's house and found about a hundred and twenty-five garden gnomes. They were all over the place. The case would generate *masses* of detections so he made it his main priority. Every morning he would go out in a CID car full of gnomes looking for houses that had some in the garden. When he found one he'd knock on the door and ask if they'd had any stolen and, if so, would they come and identify them? It was quite funny really, the CID office was full of them.

'He kept it up every day, since he got a detection for every gnome he re-housed and, after about six months, it got him a commendation. There were other people knocking themselves out on really serious cases but getting naff all, while this bloke was a hero as far as management was concerned. In the end he was telling people to say the gnomes were theirs just so he could get shot of them!

'It sounds ridiculous, but it happened, and so did other cases like it; difficult cases like rape were put to one side, in order to get more detections by catching shoplifters with plenty of previous form which you could get "taken into consideration". It was madness. I did suggest the gnome thing for Chris, actually; I thought it might have been fun to put that in for him.'

At least it would be a case that Chris could handle…

Steve agrees. 'Yes, God knows how he got in;

his DCI would have eaten him alive back then. He must have been a mason!'

All of which only confirms how crucial it is to have someone like Steve on the team. If the writers of *Life On Mars* had invented The Case of the Stolen Garden Gnomes, no-one would ever believe that it could have been true.

Part of what gives *Life On Mars* both its rich vein of humour and its dramatic tension is the clash of policing styles between Sam, with his present-day sensibilities and his reliance on hi-tech back-up, and Gene, all shoot- first-and-ask-questions-later. Or preferably, don't ask questions, full stop.

Within this framework the show has touched on a raft of issues revolving around the differences in policing then and now. Forensics: how on earth *did* cases get solved without computer databases and DNA testing? Planted evidence: can it ever be morally justified if it is used to put genuine gangsters away? Corruption and backhanders: oiling the wheels or a rotten core that has to be rooted out? Hushing up a death in custody: good PR or bad? The authenticity of the situations Sam finds himself dealing with – and the authenticity of his 1973 colleagues – is what gives the problems he has to confront their punch. And for much of that, *Life On Mars* has to thank Detective Inspector Steve Crimmins.

Lazy days, August sun beating off the reflective surface of pearlescent-beige Cortina bonnets while children chase the tin metal jangle of Ice Cream vans.

In the open-plan office of CID 'A' Division, the only sign of summer was a hammered fan grinding slow and redundant revolutions, pushing a soup of Player's smoke and second-hand Brut back and forth. Somewhere a radio shouted to nobody in particular, Lou Reed was 'Waiting For The Man'.

DC Chris Skelton stared dejectedly at the sweaty slab of corned beef in his wilting sandwich and sighed. It had the texture of an octogenarian hooker's boiled thigh. He took an experimental bite, then filed it with the day's reports while looking for a place to spit.

'Right!' he heard DCI Gene Hunt shout from somewhere to his left. He swallowed on reflex and looked over to where his superiors were talking to a couple of blokes. Called 'emselves writers when they came in. *Probably want to do some sort of book*, he thought to himself, proud of his deduction skills, though what business that was of the CID was beyond him. Probably that 'artistic licence' thing that writers always go on about.

'So, let me get this straight,' Hunt was saying, sitting himself on the corner of the desk and looking over the sheaf of documentation that – dear God – seemed to give these two the run of the place. DI Sam Tyler leaned back in his chair to give his boss room, rolling his eyes as he did so. 'You two nonces are writing a book about us?'

Adams sighed and leaned away from the smell of last night's single malt. Or maybe even this morning's. Difficult to tell with Hunt.

'Yeah, but don't worry, it'll have some pictures in it too, you should be able to follow it.'

Tyler smiled slightly, noticing the shorter man kick his colleague under the desk.

'Is that right?' Hunt sneered through yellow teeth. 'Well, that's good then, 'cos I like pictures, don't I? Except when the dozy bastards put the staples where the tits are.'

'Erm … It's not really that sort of book.' Thompson said, looking like he might bolt for cover at any second; maybe cram himself into a filing cabinet until he heard the all clear.

'No?' said Hunt.

'No… no tits involved really.'

Hunt leaned in closer, nose to nose, a spray of condensation on the smaller man's glasses. 'You could've fooled *me*.'

'We have full access to all your resources and you're to allow us interview time with any and all officers we request,' Adams replied, 'authorised, signed and rubber-stamped by the District Commissioner.'

Adams reached for the open pack of fags on the desk but pulled his fingers back quickly as Hunt tried to break his knuckles with a paperweight. 'We'll try not to be too underfoot.' He added.

'You won't even know we're here,' said Thompson, 'just part of the office furniture.'

'Oh yeah … ' Hunt smiled. 'By the end of the week I'll have probably grown so fond of you I'll have given you deputy badges.' He scrunched the signed forms in his hand. 'Or mistaken you for one of our filing cabinets and shoved this up you.'

'Filed under Police Brutality cross-referenced with Belligerent Tosser.' Adams smiled, aware that everybody was staring at him, 'I know, I have a neat turn of phrase, what can I say? I'm a writer.'

'You're a gobshite.' Hunt hissed, reaching for another fag.

'That too.' Adams was quicker this time and nicked a cigarette from the pack before Hunt could stop him. 'So,' he said, while lighting it from Hunt's begrudgingly offered match, 'where can we set up an office then?'

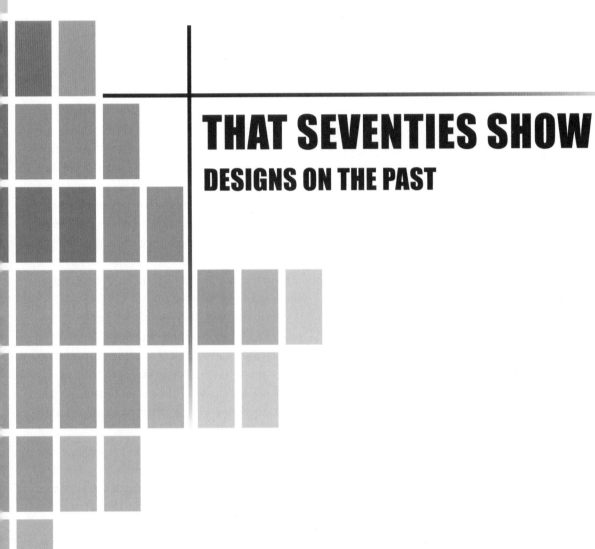

# THAT SEVENTIES SHOW
## DESIGNS ON THE PAST

Designing for television, can, like make-up and costume, be a thankless task. In the case of most mainstream contemporary dramas your job is to make everything as real, as *normal*, as possible. Therefore, if it stands out a mile you've got it wrong. A successful design, almost by definition, is one that doesn't draw the attention.

*Life On Mars* is an exception. From the very beginning the show's placement in 1973 was a key part of its strength, and the creation of that 'world' was as vital to a successful production as the casting.

'It's a period drama, and quite a *complex* period drama,' admits Brian Sykes, the show's designer, 'because it's not a period that's really been used before. It's also a lot subtler than people imagine.' There was an absolute determination at all levels to avoid the usual seventies clichés, the clashing colours and the loud décor. That's the cartoon; the false memory of the period, and nothing could be more removed from the truth.

'We looked at news reports,' explains Brian. 'We looked at Britain, the three-day week; what sort of money they had and all of a sudden it started to click – *that* was what it was like.'

'There are loads of American films from that early seventies period that are really strong visually as well,' adds Matt Gant, art director and Brian's right-hand man on the first series, 'most of them based in cities that have rather deprived areas, much as Manchester did then, post-war – it's got that kind of backdrop of desperation.'

'It's such a different culture really,' Brian continues, 'surprisingly austere, especially in Manchester. It was a desolate town, very little going on. When you walk through it now there is so much happening, so much to do. Then it was completely

*This Page (from top): Concrete structures such as the National Theatre were referenced for the ceiling of the CID set. Even detail such as the rubber expansion joints was transferred to the set build.*

*Real-life versions of the narrow windows and wall-mounted heaters both recreated in the CID 'A' Division set.*

*Corrugated concrete as seen on the undressed location used for the front desk scenes was recreated in the studio to help continuity.*

*Exterior and Interior shots of the building that provided the main inspiration for the CID set – a massive concrete structure with narrow windows allegedly capable of withstanding a nuclear blast.*

different… Wimpy was a big night out!

'The whole concept of construction is different today, too; we were so into building mega-structures then, everything had to be as big and bold as possible. If we wanted to send a man to the moon we would build a bloody *huge* rocket to do it – whereas now we are more into looking inside ourselves, making everything as *small* as we can, microchips and so on: that's where the police station came from really, making that big statement.'

'We looked at an old Barclays bank that was built in the sixties,' Matt explains, 'where they used to keep their mainframe computers – huge things in those days that took up whole floors of buildings. We were going to use that for a location but the costs of shooting out there were prohibitive. So we had to build it in Manchester, but we kept a lot of the features, like the slit windows…'

'Police stations were built like fortresses then,' says Brian, 'and you need to show that: the long thin windows, the concrete structure and the very narrow way in. These places were built at the height of the Cold War; it was hoped they could withstand a nuclear holocaust so that the country's infrastructure could be maintained. They were of a time, and once you have that in your head, the rest comes naturally.'

'We didn't look at car parks,' says Matt, aware of the received

**"Construction is different today; we were into building mega-structures then, everything had to be as big and bold as possible"**

***Above + Below:***
*Real CID office locations and props were used as a reference for set dressings for the show*

wisdom frequently found online that suggests the CID headquarters was based on – or even *shot in* according to some sources – an underground car park. 'But that structure of a concrete ceiling was something we wanted to get in. Most ceilings were made like that, but now we would have a suspended ceiling hanging beneath it so it wouldn't show. It gives it that severe, brutish feeling. You don't want that place to feel comfortable at all; it has to feel like you couldn't relax there. I took a lot of reference photos at the South Bank in London, buildings like the National Film Theatre, the Barbican, those pre-cast concrete buildings where you can see the marks of the wood used to mould it: that textured look. The back wall in the CID office was referenced from that. Then there's a very distinctive ribbed concrete effect that wasn't going to be used originally. But having found a big county office building in Stockport which we loved as the exterior, and which features that effect, we added it to tie the two sets together; so when you cut between the two it's just another visual element, which makes you believe it's part of the same building.'

The lighting was a creative solution to a logistical problem, thanks largely to director of photography Adam Suschitzky. Matt explains: 'There was an ongoing discussion about the

**Above:** Brian Sykes' original concept sketch in charcoal of the CID offices

**Below + Right:** Models of major sets are often made to aid set construction and give the production team a better idea of the finished product. This CID model shows the extent of the full set and its lack of parallel lines. With the ceiling in place, the model could also be used to judge how it would appear on screen (right) by taking photos from within the model. The real set entirely fills the studio, with only limited space to access the lighting behind each of the walls.

**Opposite Top:** The CID ceiling, constructed of polystyrene and wood is suspended on a custom-built grid system. It extends from one end of the set to halfway across Gene's office.

**Opposite Middle:** The CID set – empty, and fully dressed, with props and furnishings.

**Opposite Bottom:** Images from the real reception area dressed to match the era. Notice the corrugated concrete walls that were also mimicked on the actual set to help the location blend in.

# TO BUILD OR NOT TO BUILD?

With a large selection of sets and locations seen on screen, the art department, producers and locations manager will discuss each script during pre-production to decide which scenes will need to be shot on a set (requiring a build), and which scenes are best done on location.

For series one, the main CID set was constructed inside Studio A at BBC Manchester, with an adaptable format that allowed the production team to use the same space for scenes requiring the cells, the officers' locker room, the canteen and various corridors.

In the studio next door, Sam's flat and the Railway Arms shared space (with one needing to be partially dismantled to assemble the other). In television, smaller sets are usually constructed using only three walls, the fourth typically being unseen by the camera. With Sam's flat, all four walls and a ceiling were built and each wall was removed as needed when shooting to allow access to the cameras and crew. Next door to Sam's flat the Lost and Found room was constructed, utilising three of the studio's own brick walls and a fourth constructed to feature the thin horizontal window at the back.

The exterior of the CID building was shot on location at a council building in Stockport, where the art department dressed the entrance and foyer area, adding the front desk and various filing cabinets along with adjustments to the large windows and main door. Props, such as files, telephones, drawer units and typewriters from the CID studio set would often be re-used in the foyer rather than having a separate prop supply.

windows because we'd used every inch of floor space that we could for the set, determined to make it as big as possible; the result being we couldn't fit a useful backdrop there, a cityscape or something. So the windows are bleached out by blasting a lot of light through them: it's very stylised, with all the smoke and shards of light. You never really see anything outside. We put the blinds there to disguise the fact that there's nothing out there except big lights. Adam shone the lights right into the lens which is a really nice look, it flares a lot. Steven Spielberg used it in *Catch Me If You Can* – a film we referenced quite a bit, the FBI office in particular – where he was shining lights directly through windows. An odd thing to do, but it creates a nice surreal feeling.'

Bharat Nalluri concurs: 'The office that Tom Hanks hangs out in in that movie stuck in Brian's and my head and we played with the idea a little. I told him that I wanted to get inside Sam's perspective – he's *disorientated* so there's no parallel lines, everything clashes against each other; this is no square room with a door. The desks go in a different direction to the lights, which go in a different direction to the wall which goes in a different direction to the corridor… you never get a matching straight line.'

'We did have a few teething problems with the set,' Matt admits. 'Originally the doors were going to swing both ways on bomber hinges but because the doors are attached to quite thin partitioning, which is only anchored to the floor, the bomber hinges had such tension in them that when they swung back the whole partition swung like a sail. We tried changing them for standard hinges, but we still had a lot of wobble. If you look at the set there are some big grey heaters that are attached to the walls – they look good actually, a wonderful piece of detail, but they're only there so that the walls don't wobble all over the shop every time someone walks in the office.'

Was there ever a concern that the CID office would be too grey, too ugly?

'There were slight reservations about it,' Brian admits, 'but you have to keep true to the soul of the piece. We went for that brown tone throughout rather than any leaping colours. The colours just weren't as vibrant then; cars weren't as bright, everything was more muted. Also, if you look back at the films of the day like *Get Carter* and *All the President's*

> **"If you look back at the films of the day like *Get Carter* and *All the President's Men*, there is a sort of severity to the look of them. We wanted to emulate that"**

# WHEN IS CID NOT CID?

The main CID set encompasses an entire studio, so there is very little room for additional sets. By using extra walls (known as 'flats') and set dressings the production team can turn the back of the CID set behind Gene Hunt's office into the collator's den (above, top) the map/radio room (above, middle), the locker room, the cells or even the canteen (right). As all the rooms are inside the same (fictional) police station, fixtures and fittings (such as doors, windows and walls) would be the same throughout the building.

*Men*, there is a sort of severity to them. We wanted to emulate that, especially in the first two episodes Bharat shot. There wasn't the same amount of camera movement in those days – everything was framed up and people acted within it: there wasn't the cutting there is today, cutting from one person to another all the time.

'We couldn't do that too much because people would subconsciously reject it, but the sets were designed very carefully so that you could always feature something within the shot, interesting roof structures for example – although, again, shooting at a low angle so you can see the roof is not a modern way of shooting.

'You do have to remember though,' Brian concludes, 'that this was never going to be a show about gimmicks, like space hoppers or chopper bikes – it was a show about people and presented accordingly.'

It seems that films of the era were used very extensively as a touchstone for the design team, a visual starting point from which to work from.

'Film references are useful' agrees Matt, 'we had a list of the more obvious titles and a whole wall of printed screen grabs which really helped when new directors came in; it got the tone across straight away. They could see the set and we could talk about it, but seeing a whole wall of iconic images meant that we were all speaking the same visual language before we even began. We were able to communicate the look of the show very quickly.'

There was one visual reference that was swiftly vetoed, however:

'The producer and the director were very hot on us not using *The Sweeney*,' says Brian. 'They felt we could have fallen into the trap of being gimmicky. At the time I probably thought they were being snobbish, but looking back I realize they were quite right, we could wandered into clichés very easily.'

Another one of the challenges for the design team was the need to create a number of smaller sets for the 'hallucinations' Sam suffers.

'There is a lot of stuff that happens on the television in *Life On Mars*,' agrees Matt, 'they're not sets the audience 'inhabit', they're only seen on a screen, so you have to make a choice about how much to spend. You could treat it as another whole set and spend as much as you normally would but we'd go over budget rather rapidly.

'We did a shoot in the first series for the Test Card Girl, using a very rough internet picture of the original test card. We knocked up a version of it on the computer and then played it back on the telly. We got emails from people who actually worked for the BBC, saying it was the wrong card – the girl was different – and would we like the real one!

## TX SCRIPT EXTRACT

**PHYLLIS:** I've got a reported stabbing.
*On hearing these words GENE wakes at once.*
**GENE:** Stabbing? Where?
**PHYLLIS:** Crester's Textiles, Queen Mary Road. Uniform's already on the scene.
*GENE unwraps his butty and throws the wrapper out the window.*
**SAM:** Queen Mary Road?
*GENE grabs the handset from SAM*
**GENE:** Alpha One, we're all over it.
*He starts the car, cramming the bacon roll in his mouth. CLOSE-UP of the Cortina's exhaust and badges/logos.*
**SAM:** This is a one-way street, so just take a left and then-
*GENE nods at SAM and totally ignores his instructions. He slams the Cortina into reverse and backs out of the one-way street at full speed. SAM grabs the dash. In its haste, the car knocks over a pile of cardboard boxes stacked up in the street. SAM holds on, petrified. GENE raises his eyebrows at him, butty still hanging out his mouth.*

*The Cortina screeches down the end of the street and does a handbrake turn at the end.*

GENE DRIVES CAR
FAST. 'BACKWARD'

BACK OF CAR.

TOP SHT

CRASHES INTO
BOXES

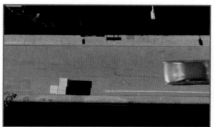

# BEAUTY IS IN THE DETAIL

Just some of the detail, researched, planned and arranged by the art department and props teams – including Gene's Gary Cooper poster, Chris's Buster comic and a large quantity of pornography, each of which can be found on the CID set.

'Then there was Mr Sockley! [the fictitious children's telly character in Episode Four] He was very popular as it happens; everyone wanted him to come back. He was a pretty instant creation because we wanted a character from a real children's show, but we had issues getting the rights cleared.'

What was the greatest difficulty for the design department?

'Controlling things on location,' Brian answers. 'Because of the demands of the script, our characters have to inhabit the world of the seventies outside – which seems obvious, but it's a real headache for the designer. A closed set is one thing but here you have people driving or walking around all the time, and everything the audience sees needs to be consistent with the era. When you start looking into it you realize that the world has changed so much. There's more stuff to buy now, more choice, more colour; you realize that you're going to find it really bloody difficult to get back to the soul of the seventies. Everything's different: every bit of street furniture; everyone's houses have UPVC windows, there's rubbish lying in the streets, bin bags, satellite dishes, alarms…

'All we could do was camouflage things. We had plastic brickwork to cover alarms and satellite dishes; vast amounts of brown masking tape to disguise new windows. Everyone does things to their houses these days. The idea of DIY was much less widespread in the seventies: unless you had money you didn't go out and paint your house or put on a new gate or change all your window

**Above:** *Children's TV character Mr Sockley, created especially for the show, seen here with his co-host – a rare appearance in front of the camera by John McKay, director of Episodes Three and Four.*

frames. Everything you look at now is wrong. There are a few streets around Manchester that haven't been developed, but they are few and far between.

'Another thing you notice from photos is the vast amount of waste land there was at that time; undeveloped bomb-damaged terraces that had been knocked down and left. Not many places in Britain today have that sort of barren waste land, so it's a struggle to represent that. If you were doing a much older period drama, set in Georgian times for example, it would actually be easier – you would just go to the classic cities like Bath or Bristol. But in *Life On Mars*, characters are driving around streets that have to look believable. At the same time everybody's got a logo, shop windows are full of goods, and you're always trying to hide all that. That was definitely the hardest thing.'

Difficult or not, it's obvious that the challenges of *Life On Mars* fired the creativity of the design team. Will the experience have spoilt them for working on more conventional dramas?

'There is a lot of variety in what we do here,' Matt admits. 'I wouldn't say it's spoilt other jobs but it will certainly make me hunt for a different approach in future projects. I think there is room for strong visuals in any drama: a lot of the more stylized ideas we developed here would translate into other shows – although we'd have to water them down slightly. It's a stimulating show, very visual and a lot of fun with the seventies stuff – the props and the cars. When the actors walk on set in their costumes it brings life into what we've done. What's nice is that even though people have memories of the seventies it's always a subjective memory, so I think *Life On Mars* has, in some ways *influenced* people's memories: they will look at it and remember things.

'It's not perfect, we've bent the rules a bit sometimes – you're creating a feel for a *drama* not a documentary. I'm more interested in creating the atmosphere to back up a story than in making everything perfect. There are always things we can't afford to build or remove…we don't have the time or the money to make it in that much detail, so it's an *impression* of the seventies. A lot of people who have come to work on the show have expected it to have been made on a much higher budget than it was. It's shot very well; it's lit very well, the performances are incredible; so it stands up and looks like more money than it is. Everyone has worked really hard to make it as slick as it can be. But we beg, borrow and steal to make things work and the only thing that's really important is what ends up on screen.'

> **"It's a stimulating show, very visual and a lot of fun with the seventies stuff – the props, the cars. When the actors walk on set in their costumes it brings life into what we've done."**

*SJ Clarkson, director of Episodes Five and Seven, is a strong believer in planning shots using storyboards. This sequence from Episode Five shows how closely shots can be planned, with the original sketches from Brian Sykes (this page) and the completed sequence (opposite page).*

**EXT. MANCHESTER STREET.**
*Ford Capri screams around corner with GENE's Cortina literally on its tail. GENE driving, SAM holding on for his life. They turn around another bend, and another. The Capri tears onto a football pitch - the two teams scatter as the cars carve their way across the pitch. One MAN dives to the floor for safety. The REFEREE just dodges out of the way in time.*

**GENE** (out of window): Oi referee! Are you blind?
*The Capri turns at the far end of the pitch and heads back towards other goal, the players dodging out the way again.*

**GENE:** Right, Hold on!

**SAM:** (holding on) What d'you think I'm doing?
*GENE spins the car around and he's on the Capri's tail again.*

**GENE:** Back of the net!
*The Capri is heading straight for the goal net. The GOAL KEEPER ducks out just in time as the Capri spins horizontally into the goal, coming to a halt in a mess of broken uprights and goal net. GENE's Cortina pulls up right in front. A marked Police car and a second unmarked car stop nearby. As GENE & SAM get out the car CHRIS and RAY get out of the unmarked car. They join GENE and SAM as they approach the Capri.*

**GENE:** D'you see that?

**RAY:** Definitely offside.

**GENE:** (To YOUNG MAN in the Capri) You're nicked sunbeam.

**SAM:** (Pulling YOUNG MAN out of the car) Come on. Chris, take him away, charge him.
*Just then CHRIS trips and gets himself all tangled up in the goal net.*

**RAY:** I'll do it.
*RAY grabs the YOUNG MAN and pushes him up against the car.*

**RAY:** I'm arresting you for theft of a motor vehicle, resisting arrest and driving like a div.

# LIFE ON MARS?
## Muse-ical influences

There can be no doubt that, alongside the design and costumes, the use of period music in *Life on Mars* helped cement the atmosphere of 1973 in the minds of every viewer. From Cream to Led Zeppelin, Pink Floyd to (*ahem*) Roger Whittaker, the finished episodes exude early seventies culture from every frame and couldn't be more evocative of the era if they'd put on a pair of platform boots and started guzzling Spangles.

Barney Pilling, the editor on the first two episodes, was the man selected to set the musical standard. 'The track 'Life on Mars?' was already in place,' he tells us, 'but the rest of it was pretty much my fault: the hard time the clearance department had was definitely down to me!'

Most dramas would have shied away from such extensive use of copyrighted music, since paying for it eats into the budget like nobody's business. However, there was a deliberate drive to make *Life On Mars* different and Barney's work was very much a part of that.

'When I read the script it was wonderful and fantastic but had no real blueprint of how to achieve what was needed. With many programmes you can draw on influences – which Bharat did to create the look of it – but it's a wonderful thing being part of a show that's finding its personality.

'I was actually born in 1973 so a lot of research was needed, but then that's one of the main things I love about my job: I spend a lot of time and money listening to music.'

So how did he start the process of nailing down the sound of *Life On Mars*?

'We did a promotional film for the series early on and I put 'Ace of Spades' by Motorhead over a montage of Gene Hunt thumping people, which worked absolutely beautifully. It had an attitude to it; it was just so perfect for him. But that track was from the eighties, so we couldn't use it. Instead I traced back through punk and the New York Dolls and Blue Oyster Cult – bands which were useable – hunting for things that were in the right time frame and which had that vibe. Anything with *attitude* was fair game, that was my general system.

'I have to say I turned up some great music that I never would have listened to or bought. The Who in particular. I'd never heard 'Baba O'Riley' before – the track used so effectively during the street scene outside the record shop in Episode One, which is also the theme tune to *CSI: NY*, for those who like their trivia. I'm from an electronic music background, so none of it was really stuff I'd listened to before, but that track blew me away. Where had they been? If I'd been around at the time they were the band I'd have been listening to, because they had that really epic feel to them. Originally I'd used that track over the closing scene – when Sam is stood on the roof, wondering whether to jump. I put it over that sequence because, to be honest, it was my favourite of all the tracks I'd come across, so I wanted to put it over the most climactic moment in the show. But it was too big for that

> "*Live and Let Die was Matthew Graham's suggestion. He hadn't put it in the script but he threw the title up as an idea, and when I tried it it was blinking genius. It really works.*"

# GREETINGS, POP PICKERS!

1973 saw some phenomenally successful albums released, including both Mike Oldfield's *Tubular Bells* and Pink Floyd's *Dark Side of the Moon* - both of which spent several years in the the top forty, but didn't hit the top spot until 1974. Below are the UK number one albums from 1973, excluding compilations...

**JANUARY**
SLADE – *Slayed*
GILBERT O'SULLIVAN – *Back to Front*
**FEBRUARY**
ELTON JOHN – *Don't Shoot Me, I'm Only the Piano Player*
**MARCH**
ALICE COOPER – *Billion Dollar Babies*
**APRIL**
LED ZEPPELIN – *Houses of the Holy*
THE FACES – *Ooh La La*
**MAY**
DAVID BOWIE – *Aladdin Sane*
**AUGUST**
PETERS + LEE –*We Can Make It*
**SEPTEMBER**
ROD STEWART – *Say It Again Rod*
THE ROLLING STONES – *Goat's Head Soup*
**OCTOBER**
SLADE – *Sladest*
STATUS QUO – *Hello*
**NOVEMBER**
DAVID BOWIE – *Pin Ups*
**DECEMBER**
ROXY MUSIC – *Stranded*
DAVID CASSIDY – *Dreams Are Nothin' More Than Wishes*
ELTON JOHN – *Goodbye Yellow Brick Road*

# DID YOU HEAR THAT?

Baba O'Riley by The Who
Episode One

Live And Let Die by Wings
Episode Two

Ballroom Blitz by Sweet
Episode Three

Jean Genie by David Bowie
Episode Four

White Room by Cream
Episode Five

Wonderful World by Louis Armstrong
Episode Six

Toxic by Britney Spears
Episode Seven

Devil's Answer by Atomic Rooster
Episode Eight

scene; the action and music were working against each other. I was determined to get it in somewhere, though, and Bharat suggested we shift it to the street scene where, with a bit of re-editing, it worked brilliantly.'

There's another musical highlight at the start of the second episode where 'Live and Let Die' by Paul McCartney and Wings combines with the sight of our heroes running around in swimming trunks to glorious effect.

'That was Matthew Graham's suggestion. He hadn't put it in the script but he threw the title up as an idea, and when I tried it it was blinking genius. It really works. We didn't think for a million years we'd get clearance, but the track worked so well that I just went ahead and did it; I didn't listen to the people who said we wouldn't be able to clear it. Let everybody fall in love with it once it's in place and they'll all try that much harder to make sure it stays!'

In fact it was only when producer Claire Parker wrote personally to Sir Paul McCartney and sent him the sequence for which they wanted to use the song that they got permission. Such determination must have cost everyone a sleepless night or two…

'We wanted the opening episodes to have real punch. But I got everything in that I wanted – for the UK release anyway. I had one Lou Reed track that we lost worldwide.'

Barney's initial unfamiliarity with the seventies music scene was an advantage, enabling him to approach it with a fresh ear and avoid any musical clichés. 'Not coming from that era did mean that I didn't just look to the obvious hits. It didn't become a playlist of tracks that you hear all the time on seventies compilations: there's a lot of album tracks in there, alongside the big favourites. If it worked and I liked it was game on really, that was my only rule.'

Yet, important as they were, the tracks he chose were not the only elements to the music of *Life On Mars*. Once they were in place it was time to build in the specially commissioned score – both the main theme and the incidental music – which was both composed and arranged by Edmund Butt.

'The 1973 tracks worked brilliantly alongside

> **"Instead of going for what might have seemed the obvious choice of pastiche seventies sound, Ed Butt used a much more contemporary approach to reflect the fact that Sam is from the present day"**

Ed's beautiful music,' comments Claire Parker. 'Instead of going for what might have seemed the obvious choice of pastiche seventies sound, Ed used a much more contemporary approach to reflect the fact that Sam is from the present day.' Thus, the two different styles of music provide a counterpoint not just to each other, but to the two very different realities of Sam's life – further fine testament to the attention to detail with which *Life On Mars* was made.

## LIFE ON MARS?

Bowie's song originally appeared on the album *Hunky Dory* in 1971 – alongside the now equally famous 'Changes' – but it wasn't released as a single until 1973, after Ziggy had made him star. While the lyrics tell the story of a girl hiding in a cinema after an argument with her parents, the song was actually written as an ironic response to a failed writing commission he'd done a few years earlier. In 1968 Bowie had written English lyrics for a 1967 French song called 'Comme D'Habitude', calling his version 'Even a Fool Learns to Love'. It wasn't great, as Bowie himself has admitted, and was never released. Paul Anka then bought the rights to 'Comme D'Habitude' and set about writing his own English version. His was more successful; it's most famous recording was by Frank Sinatra. It was called 'My Way'.

The chords of 'Life on Mars?' and 'My Way' are intentionally similar and Bowie added the note 'inspired by Frankie' on the album sleeve as a wink to the other song's best known performer.

# 1973 – THE RETIREMENT GIG

*'Everybody … This has been one of the greatest tours of our life … Of all the shows on this tour this particular show will remain with us the longest, because … not only is it … not only is it the last show of the tour, but it's the last show that we'll ever do. Thank you.'* DAVID BOWIE 3 July 1973

*'And that was that really.'* DAVID BOWIE in 2002 from the book **Moonage Daydream.**

There could be no question that those gathered at the Hammersmith Odeon on the last night of Bowie's epic tour as his alter ego Ziggy Stardust were a little taken aback by this closing statement.

They weren't the only ones surprised by Bowie's speech. The band – the *Spiders from Mars* – were shocked as well. Having had made a speedy transition from jobbing session musicians to part of a musical phenomenon, they had had no warning that it might all as suddenly be over.

Both *The Rise and Fall of Ziggy Stardust and the Spiders from Mars* (1972) and its follow-up *Aladdin Sane (1973)* had been hugely successful, the latter being Bowie's first UK number one and one of the fastest-selling albums of its time. That summer Bowie had five albums in the chart concurrently, a position they would hold for nineteen weeks. The 'Life on Mars?' single had also just entered the top three.

As it turned out Bowie was simply 'retiring' Ziggy, driven by his creative urge to move on to new personas and styles. It was eighteen months of blinding fame but enough was enough. Interviewed later he said: 'It was almost as if I was following a pattern of what I had written, because I was in that frame of mind that this had to be done. Ziggy broke up the band so I had to do it too.'

### The Gene Genie/Jean Genie

Gene Hunt's nickname of The Gene Genie is a p[...] David Bowie track 'Jean Genie' from the album 19[...] Sane. The track title in turn is a reference to French [...] Genet, whose works include *The Thief's Journal* (19[...] *Lady of the Flowers* (1944). Interestingly, Genet spe[...] years as a petty thief and prostitute, writing his [...] prison for offences including vagabondage and l[...]

# PIMP MY THREADS
## Emma Rosenthal – Costume Designer

It's a common theme in the production of *Life On Mars*: that 'children in a sandpit' feeling of both cast and crew relishing the challenges that a show set in 1973 has to offer. From Barney Pilling being paid to increase his seventies rock collection to Bharat Nalluri reliving his Newcastle childhood, there's no doubting the enthusiasm for this act of recreation. This is never more evident than when speaking to Emma Rosenthal, the head of the costume department. Could it be regarded as healthy, this love of the flared trouser and the kipper tie? You mean to say that she *likes* seventies fashion?

'I do now! I don't necessarily like the fabrics though, working in the heat of summer wearing clothes made of nylon.'

She doesn't regard the seventies as ugly?

'The eighties were worse! Plus, you've got to remember that in the early seventies people were actually still wearing clothes from the late sixties. Fashion was expensive then, you didn't just pop down to New Look for a new outfit. Many people wore hand-me-downs. When I was a child a lot of my clothes were second hand; I had three cousins and the clothes would pass down through them to my sister and then to me. We wouldn't dream of doing that now. Everything's much more disposable. I have to say, though, I have developed a taste for the clothes… The amount of times I've said to my mates, "I love that dress!" They just look at me like I'm bonkers.'

Nor is she alone in her enthusiasm.

'When I first fitted Dean [Andrews – DS Ray Carling] he liked his outfit so much he asked if he could wear the one he had on for the whole series!'

There was some talk of costume rebellion, however:

'When I had my first interview with Claire Parker and the writers, everyone wanted Sam to do something with his costume. They said that if he was a man from the present day who had woken up in these 1973 clothes, wouldn't he have hated them and trimmed the collars or something? We didn't do that in the end. Mind you, no-one ever questions where Sam got his clothes from; he just wakes up with them. Perhaps his subconscious makes sure he looks a bit cooler than everyone else. He doesn't wear nylon or polyester, it's cotton all the way!'

Gene Hunt has a look all his own, too.

'He has several different shirts and suits but people don't notice that. It's difficult to see beyond the coat. That look came straight from the original script: Sam wore leather and Gene wore the big car coat. It works well though; that coat is pure Gene.'

As are the trademark white leather loafers; a distinctive set of footwear, to be sure.

'When I first showed them to Claire, she thought I was joking. "Why not?" she said, not entirely seriously…'

For a woman who originally graduated in geography, costume must seem a strange way to earn a living.

'Absolutely. I was always really

> **"When I first showed Gene's loafers to Claire Parker she thought I was joking! 'Why not?' she said, not entirely serious…"**

into it, though. I did makeup for school productions and one year my teacher asked if I could sew. We did *The Sound of Music* and I organized all the costumes. *I can do this*, I thought, though it never occurred to me that it would be my career, which is why I still did a geography degree. But I managed to get some work experience at the Royal Exchange Theatre and decided to do an intensive one-year costuming course once I'd graduated. After that I got a job at a London theatre and that was that. I've worked at the Old Vic, the National, the Globe, the RSC and lots of telly over the last eight years.'

Falling as it does somewhere between contemporary and historical costume, *Life On Mars* must have caused Emma a fair

**Above:** *Rack upon rack of seventies-style clothes fill two trailers – some of it vintage clothing, some modern-day equivalents and a handful of hire costumes. From patterned polyester to cool cuban heels, Emma Rosenthal (pictured bottom right) and her team have helped seal the seventies look on screen for all the cast and background artists.*

share of headaches, sourcing so many authentic seventies clothes. You can't just pick them up from the high street – seventies revivals not withstanding – and you're not going to get them from a historical costumiers either.

'The extras are the thing; in most modern dramas you would simply ask them to turn up wearing a certain type of outfit, but I have to kit them all out. Not that they get much choice: it's like dressing models, they come in and I put the clothes on them. Sizing is also a problem. We've got so much bigger these days, because of our diet mainly – junk food is much more plentiful than it was then. A lot of the genuine seventies clothes that I use are very small and it can be a struggle getting some of the actors into them. I do have to cheat a bit and use modern clothes that have a seventies style, not only to get the right sizes but also so that I can double – sometimes triple – up. If you're filming an episode which takes place over one day you can't expect the actor to wear the same shirt for the several weeks it takes to shoot it. But with the early start and late finish, we don't want to have to wash everything nightly either, so you make sure that there are identical outfits in order for you to rotate them.'

So popping out to New Look is something she's been known to do herself?

'I'm lucky because I've been designing in Manchester for nearly six years so I've got plenty of contacts here. I also have a good relationship with a hire company in Bristol – I've got seventy police uniforms on hire for twenty-six weeks so they do me a very preferential rate. I do get a lot of discounts and, to be honest, the retro shops in Manchester are very good, much cheaper than in London.

**"Ultimately for me if the actors are happy that makes a big difference; you don't want them walking on set saying, 'God, I hate my costume.' "**

'It always comes down to what's a better use of money; is it cheaper to buy or hire? I use every trick I know to keep it all within budget. I did get excited at the end of the series though when I read about the wedding in the script. I said to the director, "Two hundred extras, let me do a huge wedding!" but it got down to thirty floating around. We didn't even have a bride!'

How much of the decision-making rests on her shoulders? Is it always a group discussion or is she left pretty much to her own devices?

'A bit of both: we have lots of meetings; the producers, the directors and then the actors. The casting's always the major factor. I could read a script and decide a character would be terrific in hot pants but when the actor or actress comes in they could look totally wrong in them. Ultimately for me if the actors are happy that makes a big difference; you don't want them walking on set saying, "God, I hate my costume." I work with the art department a lot as well, I need to see what the sets are so I don't put actors in clothes that will clash with the wallpaper or the couch. For the main cast I take Polaroids to show the director and producers, just to make sure they're happy with them, but we don't have a long enough schedule to do that all the time so its mostly down to me.'

There's a considerable amount of pressure, then?

'I've been designing for a few years now, so it's not so bad. When I first started, I was scared every day and it's still a terrifying thought that I'm *so* responsible for everything. But ultimately I've been employed to do this job and I hope they trust me. I've never sent anything on set so terrible they've had to change it. Still, there's always tomorrow!'

**This page:** Glittered and sequined clothing began to creep in to fashion for both women and men in the early seventies as glam rock surfaced. For Episode Four Emma had to clothe dozens of people to fill the dance floor at The Warren nightclub, amongst them William Matheson as legendary rock star Marc Bolan (above, centre).

Using an array of patterned polyester fabrics (like the lime green and brown paisley and baby-pink flower patterns featured left), wide-collared shirts and suits (such as those worn below), the patrons of The Warren really do fit the bill.

# REAL/UNREAL
## Post-Production Special Effects

Huge efforts were made by the *Life On Mars* production team to recreate the detail of 1973 so that the world felt as real as they could make it. When it wasn't possible to do this through the on-set design, the CGI wizards were called in to add their magic. 'It was essential that we avoided situations where the audience could see the boundaries between 1973 and the present day,' producer Claire Parker explains. 'We always tried to maintain the illusion, so we worked with two CGI teams: Pepper, who, amongst other things, helped create the dramatic sequence when Sam first gets knocked down and the final rooftop scene in Episode One, and Manchester-based 3sixtymedia.'

What sort of shots would need CGI treatment? Matt Wood, one of the visual effects artists at 3sixtymedia, talks us through the creation of a particular example.

'When you're doing special effects for TV, you very rarely get the chance to do spaceships and dinosaurs, it's more about real people, real places and real dramas. If you're doing *Harry Potter*, it's great to have things which don't look real to jump out of the screen at you, but for us you can't get away with that – if something we do looks unreal, then chances are it's going to spoil the dramatic moment.

'The biggest scene we did for *Mars* was in Episode One, furnishing the whole street – the "teenage wasteland" shot outside the music shop. We get a 360° pan around a seventies high street with 'Baba O'Riley' playing in the background. The production team had a real street, and they were able to dress it up with some shops and scenery, but down one end of the street there were some modern features and there weren't enough shops, so we extended the street. On one corner you can see a shoe-shop; we put that in there. On the other side of the street was a pub and a café: apparently there was a problem with the electrics and they couldn't get the lights working, so we illuminated all the windows. At the back end of the shot there was a multi-storey car park – we just got rid of the whole thing and put in a cinema instead. As the original street just ended, we put another section in there to make it seem longer. There was also a modern car left parked in the street, so we removed that and replaced it with a seventies model.

'We do have the advantage that people aren't expecting computer generated imagery, they're not looking for it. Our biggest shot was a street! Not hard to shoot, you'd imagine, but when it comes down to it, trying to find a street you can film on in Manchester, that you can block off at both ends and fill with extras – it becomes quite a task.'

Was everything planned for that shot from an early stage?

'Much of the work we do for a drama is on a very tight schedule, so there isn't time to plan everything in detail. Many of the things we added were done after seeing the rushes [the daily tapes used to assess that particular day's filming]. Having seen the shot, the production team said "wouldn't it be great just to change that? Oh...and if we're changing *that*, why don't we just change *this*?" The whole idea of

> "We do have the advantage that people aren't expecting it, they're not looking for it. Our biggest shot was a street!"

*The original shot from the rushes, showing a multi-storey carpark, and a covered modern car left of frame...*

*The basic composite shot, showing the new road, cinema and 1970s car roughly in place.*

Once the basic perspectives and motion have been matched between the original footage and the visual effect, the detail is attended to, such as extreme edges of buildings, extras, and any other elements that need to be fine-tuned to better blend in with the shot, as shown by this screen capture of the process at work.

On the left is the original and on the right is the completed effects shot, where the effects artist is concentrating on the pedestrian and the car roof, ensuring they blend with the new cinema backdrop.

# BLUESCREEN/ GREENSCREEN

With post-production visual effects, using a single non-skin tone colour like green or blue as a background gives the editor or compositor an easy way to separate the foreground action (such as actors, props or models) from the real background action, and overlay it on to a specially created or separately shot collection of background elements. The most common use of this is for a weather reporter on television who is filmed against a blue screen; the blue element is then removed and replaced with a computer-generated map, which can also employ animated effects such as rain falling or moving clouds.

With the advances in computing and computer-generated visual effects, the use of bluescreen/greenscreen (also known as ChromaKey or Colour Separation Overlay/C.S.O.) has increased, with some films such as *Sky Captain and the World of Tomorrow*, *Sin City* and *The Matrix* using the process extensively to show alien landscapes, fictitious cities, gravity-defying stunts and action sequences.

The choice of colour – green or blue – is often up to the effects artists, depending on the demands of a specific shot. Green has become the preferred colour because digital video cameras pick up more green than blue, making it easier to work with and in need of less lighting.

putting the cinema in that 360° shot came from seeing the rushes and thinking, "well, it could do with a bit of work, that end of the shot, it looks a bit boring". We already had the footage scanned in and had tracked the camera movements, so why not take it a bit further and make it more entertaining? We're often there on set, talking to the directors and the directors of photography: they'll ask whether we can achieve a certain shot or not – most directors assume we can't so that if we have to say "no", they're not disappointed!'

So how early on does 3sixty get involved?

'It depends – if the director has a very specific view for a scene early on, we'll get involved at the pre-production stage. They'll ask if they can use their chosen location, do a certain shot, and still remain within budget. We may go with them on a location recce to see what's there, see if there'll be any problems, and maybe even go out when they're shooting as well. Sometimes we'll go on set so that we can check camera movements, and objects or people that are in between the camera and our effect. Lots of people walking or hair blowing in the wind means you'll need a "green screen"' [see left].

'We did another shot nearer to the end of the series, in Episode Eight, where there was a car crash. There was a car travelling up the road, and another one hit it from the side. It wasn't a planned special effects shot beforehand. They had the stunt guys in – *physical* effects – to do the whole thing but they knew they only had one chance. Two busted old cars crashing into each other: the film crew knew they weren't going to get a chance to do that again. Once shot, it didn't look *that* great – because of safety precautions and the state of the cars, the speed wasn't as fast as they'd wanted, and the result is a crash that looks like you wouldn't even get a bruise off it. So we did quite a bit of work on it – we added some CGI glass coming out of the windows, added a little door handle that comes flying off – and it still didn't quite work, so we cut the cars out of the shot and animated them so it looks like they're moving a lot faster. When the car to the left of the frame hits the main car we threw both of them over to the right, so it looks like a really hard impact. And because of that, we had to trim some of the camera shot off – panning across the screen to follow the action – which meant we had to paint in an extra bit of set too: a house, windows, some extra road.'

And people won't notice that, they'll just think it's a car crash...

'Exactly; and most of the work we do is 'fixing' problems that happen on set, as they're working so fast. We can be on set for example, and the lighting truck breaks down just inside of the shot, or someone holding their shopping walks by at the edge of the frame. It could take half an hour to move it or re-shoot it, but we can say "it's alright, we can fix that" and the team can get on and do their work.'

# COMPLETING THE EFFECT

In this scene from Episode Four, a panning (moving) camera shot follows Sam's point-of-view as he looks up at the busy entrance to The Warren nightclub, owned by gangster Stephen Warren.

This night scene was shot in Rochdale, where the art department had dressed a building entrance and placed seventies cars in shot.

Once the scene is shot, the confirmed take (pictured above) is sent to the post-production team at 3sixty where they would track the camera movements, remove the old signage and create the new neon sign, then mix the two together in a process known as compositing. The final version, as seen on screen, is shown below.

'We do 3D modelling in Maya, ' Matt continues, "and we also use MayaLive for camera tracking, which we used extensively for our effects shots in *Life On Mars*. [When you're adding an effect to something shot on a moving or handheld camera, the effect needs to match the movement of the camera to appear real. For this, special camera tracking software is used to recreate the physical camera movements in a computer environment, allowing the effects artist to effectively 'film' the digital effect with the same movements as the physical element.]

'After the camera tracking has been completed, we would take out a series of frames, and "repaint" them using Adobe Photoshop, working with digital photographs I'd taken of a street here, a shop there, and so on. These are then morphed and transformed to match in with perspectives. Those frames are then placed back in the 3D software with the matched camera moves, and the result is a panning shot. This shot is then composited back into the original shot using Fusion 5, which is similar to Shake, but is much more prevalent over in America. It's all about using the tools you're comfortable with, and we're a small team: the 360° street shot was the work of two people, myself and Tanvir Hanif; and Simon Blackledge, who's our Flame operator, also worked on a few shots later on in the series, so that's three people. We can go up to seven for a really big project with lots of shots.'

# A LOT OF WOOD

## The Cortina Mark III – 2000E

It's hardly surprising that viewers love Gene Hunt's Cortina. After all, there are many precedents: Inspector Morse's Mark Two Jaguar, Starsky's 'Striped Tomato' from *Starsky and Hutch*, Bo and Luke's General Lee from *The Dukes of Hazzard* ... TV cars have a habit of forcing themselves into the limelight. In fact, Gene's motor was just as widely embraced when Ford first released it at the Earl's Court Motor Show in 1970.

The show saw two new vehicles put before the public, both of which would become enduring icons and had the testosterone levels of a rampaging bull elephant – British Leyland's Range Rover and the Mark III Cortina from Ford.

The Cortina had always been pitched as a 'family motor' but, with the strong competition of cheap import cars from Japan, the Mark III represented Ford's attempt to regain lost sales with a little extra comfort and style.

The shape of the body-work was often referred to as 'Coke-bottle curves' and was similar to the 1968 Victor from Vauxhall.

As with previous Cortinas, Ford gleefully offered the car in many versions: thirty-five variations in all, fluctuating in their specifications both decoratively and under the bonnet. At the bottom end, budget drivers could help themselves to a 1300cc model which sounded like it had emphysema and struggled at high speeds (one road test described it as a 'sheep in wolf's clothing'). The 1600cc was the most popular, with a 2000cc model to keep the most Brut-laden of sales reps happy.

The Cortina never achieved the high masculine status in motor sport that Ford's Escort did but it was a clear hit with the British public, rapidly becoming the most popular new car in the country.

But it was with the introduction of the 2000E in 1973 that the Cortina really hit its stride. The 'E' stood for 'executive' of course, a standard marketing trick, despite the fact that anything so blatantly labelling itself as such will often be seen as the opposite. In this case, however, it found its market well: thick carpet, velour upholstery and, as the brochure pointed out: 'lots of wood'. Lovely.

Old Spice in the glove box and string-backed hands on the wheel – a real man's car was born. For a while at least. Nowadays the Cortina is rarely seen on our roads, despite its affordability in the used-car market and a worldwide network of dedicated fans. Still, it could have been worse; the Range Rover and its terrible offspring seem doomed to a life of little more than school runs and Tesco car parks. History has a marvellous way of outfoxing the advertising world.

The car used in the series was bought from a collector and has been the subject of a number of e-mails and forum postings online: most the subject of devoted drooling; a few concerning minute historical inaccuracies – most particularly with the dashboard, which would seem to have been upgraded with some 1975 trimmings.

Matthew Graham takes such things in his stride:

# Old Spice in the glove box and string-backed hands on the wheel, a real man's car was born...

'The interiors and exteriors are from the same car so it must have been modified by the previous owner... Maybe we needed more Ford freaks on the crew.'

It would seem there are quite enough already,. 'Everyone on set wanted the Ford Cortina; it became quite a coveted item,' says John Simm, 'Unfortunately I didn't get to drive it because it was Gene's car and I didn't have one, which is unfair! Hutch from *Starsky and Hutch* had a car; a *knackered* car but a car all the same. Maybe a Capri or something would be nice!'

Ironically a Capri was the first choice for Gene Hunt's car but the prop department settled for the 2000E because it was the best car they could find from that era – a lucky mistake in many ways, considering the adulation heaped on it by motor-minded viewers.

Perhaps its admirers would be a little less enamoured if they had the opportunity to drive it themselves. 'It's very difficult to handle without power steering,' according to Phillip Glenister. 'I was rather shocked by it. It's a rust bucket really so when it's not your car you tend to throw it around a bit... I was putting my foot down, slamming on the brakes and trying to hit certain marks which meant I had to do several rehearsals to get it right. I hated getting back into my car at the weekends, though, because I'd be driving with my missus and she'd say, "You're driving awfully fast dear, can you slow down? You can do it at work but this is Richmond!"'

# "Everyone on set wanted the Ford Cortina; it became quite a coveted item"

# LOST AND FOUND:
# DC CHRIS SKELTON

Lost and Found. A world of metal racking and the dispossessed. There's nothing worth having here; whenever something of even the vaguest interest passes the threshold it's snatched up before it can hit the shelf. From the desk sergeant's handbag to the radio that crackles in the canteen, Lost and Found has served a purpose and let's just say that the rear-view mirror in DC Skelton's Maxi would be a lot less fetching without the furry dice found swinging from an abandoned car in Ancoats. Nobody's ever bought an umbrella in CID – that would be silly. Waste of good beer money.

'What are you doing?' Thompson asked, staring at his colleague who was buried up to his midriff in the detritus of years of misplaced junk.

Adams looked up, a flat cap on his head and arms full of old Super 8 reels.

'Bonding with our office environment.' He sighed and dumped the reels back where he'd found them.

The door opened and DC Chris Skelton shuffled in, an advert for autumnal fabric, all deep brown and maroon.

'You wanted to see me?' He asked, in a tone of voice that only just managed to prove that he was awake.

'Yes, please grab a seat.' Thompson gestured towards an empty chair.

There was a crash from behind one of the shelf units where Adams had just found – and now broken – a selection of crockery. Who on earth leaves mugs lying around?

'Sorry,' he muttered, sticking his head around the corner of the shelf, 'butterfingers.'

Skelton sat down, awkward and uncomfortable. He tried crossing his legs in both directions before eventually putting both feet on the floor and folding his arms. 'What do you want to know then?' he asked.

'Oh, just general stuff really,' Adams reappeared from behind the shelving, still in his flat cap, and offered Skelton a cigarette. 'You know, bit of background.'

'Thanks,' Skelton took the cigarette and Adams lit it.

Skelton took a drag and exhaled with a baffled look on his face. 'Funny fag that, can't even taste it.'

'Sorry,' Adams shrugged, 'it's a "light".'

Skelton gave him a disparaging look, 'I know, saw you light it, didn't I? Just saying I can't taste 'owt that's all.'

Adams opened his mouth to explain but thought better of it.

'So, what made you want to be a policeman, then?' asked Thompson.

'Well… are you going to be talking about what we say to the others like?'

"Of course not,' Thompson replied, 'it's absolutely confidential.'

'Oh, right. Well I suppose I've always been a bit, y'know, man of action. It were always gonna be army or police really.'

Adams raised an eyebrow. 'Really?'

'Oh yeah…' Skelton leaned back in his chair, hands behind his head 'I just love danger, me. Spice o'life, in't it?'

'It certainly is … ' Adams was trying not to smirk. 'I must say you have a bearing to you that gives you away as an adventurer.'

'Yeah?' Skelton was leaning back on his chair, looking nothing of the sort.

'Definitely; a coiled spring, just waiting to snap.'

'Oh yeah… That'll be my martial arts training won't it? Jeet Kune Do. Y'know, Bruce Lee and that?' He swung his arms in a violent arc and gave a short yelp as the chair skidded from under him.

'Bloody thing,' he muttered, getting to his feet and giving the chair a kick, stubbing his toe in the process but hiding it well. 'Something wrong with the legs on that, loose or summat.'

'Cheap departmental furniture,' Thompson

offered, pointing across the room, 'try that one.'

Skelton moved over to the other chair and eyed it suspiciously for a moment before dragging it back in front of the desk and sitting down. 'I'll probably practice on it later like,' he said, gesturing over his shoulder to the upturned chair, getting a bit of confidence back, 'karate chops and that y'know?'

'Don't let us stop you.' Adams said with a smile.

Skelton looked nervously at the chair and shook his head, 'Nah… I wouldn't want to risk getting too fired up. I'm an animal when I'm roused.'

'What sort?' Adams asked before waving the question away. 'Do you find your skills make you popular with the ladies?'

'Oh yeah. Flies around… erm…' he stopped himself. 'Chocolate cake?' he finished weakly.

'Anyone permanent?' Thompson asked.

'Nah, not my style that, love 'em and leave 'em, that's me.'

'So you live on your own?'

'No, I still live with my… Yeah, on me own, that's right. Bachelor pad and that, all the mod cons… bed, kitchen… bath and… erm… stuff.'

'Sounds delightful.'

'Oh yeah… got to have somewhere good to lay your head after a hard day crimefighting, haven't you? Nice place, lovely girl… maybe a pint or two. For all I know the next shift might be my last…

'What case are you working on at the moment?' asked Thompson.

'Couple of old biddies gone doo-lally at the Co-Op, one of 'em brained the other with a tin of dog food.'

'Best let you get back to it then, Tiger.' Adams stuck his hand out to shake. 'Don't want those streets getting meaner just 'cos we've kept you talking.'

'Oh… aye, right then.' Skelton shook the proferred hand and got to his feet. 'Do you want me to send anyone else in?'

Thompson glanced at the sheets in front of him, 'You could ask DC Carling if he's not too busy.'

'Righto…' He paused in the doorway. 'And you promise you're not going to talk about any of this with the others?'

'Definitely not,' Adams smiled, 'wouldn't want to alarm them, would we?'

'Oh… good. Okay then. I'll see if Ray's free.'

He stepped out and Adams turned around, wide grin on his face. He walked over to the chair and, with a yell, gave it a half-arsed karate kick.

'Bastard!' he shouted, grabbing his now-damaged foot.

Thompson sighed, 'I'll see if anyone knows any first-aid, shall I?'

# THE OLDEST PROFESSION
## An interview with Dean Andrews + Marshall Lancaster

The red light of a Dictaphone is never an aid to relaxation, but neither Dean Andrews nor Marshall Lancaster seems unduly worried. 'Buy us a beer and you'll find us quite amenable,' says Dean. 'We're actors aren't we? *Tarts…*'

The two of them are a natural team. Yes, there are contrasts – one blond, one dark; one doing most of the talking, the other contributing dry, laconic asides – but they compliment one another, as surely as their characters, Ray Carling and Chris Skelton, represent two different sides of the seventies' CID coin.

'We always interview together,' Dean affirms, playing along. 'We find it a lot easier, we can bounce off each other.' He gestures to Marshall Lancaster. 'He can never think of anything clever to say, he's the glamour.'

Marshall smiles, happy to accept his role. They've become good friends through working on *Life On Mars* and it shows.

How did they respond to the script when they first read it?

'The concept is very unusual,' Dean reflects, 'and there's no doubt it could have fallen flat on its face. A man goes from the present day back to 1973 and finds himself surrounded by blokes with weird facial hair and sideboards … that could *easily* not have worked; but luckily, they got a great cast in us.'

They laugh and nod at one another over their pints, score one to the lads…

'It's always beautifully shot,' Dean continues. 'The writing's strong and the storyline's an interesting one. After the second and third week my mates were saying "I can't wait to find out what happens." I've never been in a show like that before, where people are begging me to tell them what happens next … that fervour's great.'

'That's the beauty about this show, you're in it for the art *and* the popularity. It's not like you're in a drama that's being watched by seven million people but it's rubbish: this is being watched by seven million and it's *quality*, critically acclaimed … you can't ask for more than that. I've been in critically acclaimed shows and I've been in publicly acclaimed shows, but getting the two things together? That comes along very rarely. To be part of that, out of all the actors in the country… You know a lot of actors would rip their arms off to be part of it.'

Not least for the chance to play such entertaining roles, too, although they need to make sure, with such clearly delineated characters – characters which could so easily fall into cliché:

the antagonist and the dozy detective – that they always remain believable as people. The script has a vital role to play but clearly the performance of the actors needs to match.

'There is some potential for cliché,' admits Dean, 'but if you're going back to the seventies that's partly where the clichés came from. You've got to look at it from a 1973 perspective and accept that it may be a cliché now but it wasn't then. Sometimes you do stop and think, "I'm playing up to the stereotype", but it's only a cliché because it's *true*; people like Ray are arseholes for a reason. Maybe they were ill-educated or maybe they were chauvinist pigs just because it *was* acceptable back then and it's the way people were. "Nice tits, make us a cup of tea!" – I do it at home, just to stay in character… the wife loves it!'

'His character's pretty funny though, really,' says Marshall. 'He wasn't necessarily written to be that way in the beginning but, well, things change; characters develop, don't they? It's the same with Chris: he's a dozy bugger but now and then he'll be the one that cracks something, or he suddenly turns on Sam when things aren't going right.'

Of course there is also the possibility that none of it is – in the strictest sense – 'real', which must allow a bit

> **"Sometimes you do stop and think, 'I'm playing up to the stereotype' but it's only a cliché because it's *true*; people like Ray are like that for a reason!"**

of scope for their characters' behaviour?

'If it *is* all in Sam's mind,' Marshall reflects, 'your characters *could* suddenly change, because if you're not real there's that dreamlike aspect where the strangest things seem normal. 'There's that scene in Episode Four where Sam's been drugged and he suddenly hears us start talking in posh doctors' voices…'

'Originally they were going to morph our heads.' adds Dean. 'Either it was too expensive or they decided that, because of our performances, they really didn't need to… Ray and Chris talking posh! That was enough really.'

'You were going to be a hyena, weren't you?' remembers Marshall, 'and I was going to be a Labrador… kind of sums up our characters!'

He changes tack, momentarily serious, although it doesn't last for long. 'Also, as an actor, you have to remember who you actually are. We're detectives, you know? We must have had something

> "Ray's a useful
> detective for giving
> 'em a smack!
> Ray'll sort 'em out!"

about us that got us in to CID in the first place… Although having said that, I've no idea how Chris did get in there…!'

Sexual favours?

'There was that,' nods Dean, mischievously. 'which he *enjoyed*. But Chris was also the only one who took Sam on, wasn't he? Then with the taping of interviews and so on, he was the only one who had the gumption to realise that that *could* work, and he's solved one or two cases because of it…'

Marshall warms to the theme of Chris's burgeoning career prospects. 'He's willing to listen, yeah … and *learn*. Whereas Ray's useful for giving 'em a smack! Ray'll sort 'em out! Get the truth out of them in five minutes … either that or kill 'em!'

Given the nature of *Life On Mars*, the story really does revolve around Sam's predicament and his relationship with Gene. Does either of them find it difficult taking a back seat in the action?

'You always want to do more,' Dean admits. 'No actor reads a script in full until he looks at

how many lines he's got. That's only natural. You wouldn't want to be a footballer without a football, you don't want to sit on the bench for Chelsea, you want to be on the pitch; everybody's the same…'

'I'd rather be a Macclesfield Town player, just for the record,' interrupts Marshall, showing me the stitched insignia on his official shirt.

'That's how sad he is,' mutters Dean, steering the conversation back to the show. 'The beauty of this production is that the two boys [Simm and Glenister] are *so good*. If there was someone you didn't rate at the front you'd be thinking, "why am I sat on the sidelines?" But they are both such great actors, you accept the show is about them and you'll get your chance every now and then.'

It's a rare actor who hasn't had to try his hand at other things to fill the gap occasionally: good reviews are all very well but they cut no ice with the bank manager. Some, of course, have different skills to fall back on…

'Singing was my career for twenty years,' explains Dean, 'but I had a lucky break five years ago which started my acting career. Now the singing's a safety net: I know that if I'm not in regular acting work I can still earn the same living I used to when I was a singer. Cruise ships, working men's clubs, casinos, holiday camps, social clubs… I did the lot. It was fun in the early days but it's a job that's going nowhere. You're not being true to yourself, because if you were true to yourself you wouldn't earn any money. If you want to do class stuff then you can perform to a room of other musicians who'll tell you how great you are, but you won't go home with a few hundred quid in your pocket."

What does he consider to be the 'class stuff'?

'Bobby Darin is my all-time hero of the male singers, Ella Fitzgerald of the females. I'm very jazz and swing orientated; I played the piano since I was six, I love those chords, augmenteds and diminisheds… I'm really not interested in those three- or five-chord wonders – for me it's Frank Sinatra, Mel Tormé; all the great swingers.

'When you're working, though, earning a living, you've got to accept that you're a jukebox for other people's taste. They come up to you at the bar saying, "sing us something we like". "How about *Dance the Night Away* by The Mavericks?" "Oh yeah, we love that…" You're a prostitute basically, prostituting a talent for financial gain."

What about Marshall? Is that how he keeps the wolf from the door in lean times? "Yeah, only for women, though, obviously; *Deuce Bigalow Macclesfield Gigolo*… When I'm not acting I do whatever I can. I did a plastering course so that I've got something to fall back on. In fact I was on the course when I heard we'd got a second series, so I didn't have to worry about the plastering for a while. Just before I got *Life On Mars*, though, I hadn't had much work for a while. I came into the audition and Bharat [Nalluri, the first director for the show] asked me what I'd done recently, so I told him I'd been doing something called "Chuck Milk On Vans". "Is that a play then?" he

"Chris is a dozy bugger, but now and then he'll be the one that cracks something"

NT. POLICE STATION/CID - NIGHT

*CLOSE-UP on a tape recorder. SAM puts the cassette in and presses 'PLAY'. He sits at his desk. CID is deserted*

CHRIS: (V.O) (THROUGH TAPE RECORDER) Interview with Billy Kemble commenced at 7.05pm.  Present are DS Ray Carling and DC Chris Skelton.

*CHRIS, ANNIE, PHYLLIS, RAY & GENE enter one by one and take their places in CID.  GENE sits on the edge of a desk near SAM, arms folded. SAM presses 'PLAY' again. The interview is now further along.*

BILLY KEMBLE: (V.O) You said I could have something to eat.

RAY: (V.O) When you tell us who gives you them drugs.

CHRIS: (V.O) That's not so difficult, is it?

*On RAY, smoking a cigarette.*

BILLY KEMBLE: (V.O) I don't know a name.  What you doing with that?

RAY: (V.O) I thought you liked it.

*RAY looks up.*

BILLY KEMBLE: (V.O) I just sell it.

*On PHYLLIS & ANNIE, both standing. ANNIE looks down.*

RAY: (V.O) Did you know that this stuff's supposed to make folk talky, Chris?

*On CHRIS, very still.*

CHRIS: (V.O) Yeah hang on mate, you can't be using that.

*On GENE.*

RAY: (V.O) I promised the guv a result.  I'm not letting him down. Give us a hand here.

*On GENE, he breaths heavily.*

BILLY KEMBLE: (V.O) Oh no, no!  I...I don't want it!

CHRIS: (V.O) I'm not sure we should

be...

RAY: (V.O) Don't you wanna be a good copper?

CHRIS: (V.O) Yeah, but you can't...

*On RAY.  We hear him raise his voice, get angry.*

RAY: (V.O) So let's get him talking. We're running out of time.

BILLY KEMBLE: (V.O) No, no don't... Please... No... Stop...!

RAY: (V.O) Now let's see what you've gotta say for yourself.

*BILLY KEMBLE'S voice is muffled, but the sound of a struggle continues. And then stops.*

BILLY KEMBLE: (V.O)No.... You can't do that.... Please!

*SAM stops the tape with a clunk. He stares, arms folded.*

SAM: Fifty minutes later Billy Kemble **was dead.**

asks. "Nah…" I said, "I've been chucking milk on vans." I'd been up all the previous night loading the lorries at the dairy. Living like an owl, up all night heaving milk…

Dean has also had his share of the contradictions of acting. 'I went to the BAFTAs,' he recalls. 'I was involved in a film that was up for one; lovely night, sat there along with Sir Michael Gambon, Joan Collins, Michael Parkinson … then the very next night I'm doing three half-hour sets at a club in Rotherham being told "if thee don't fill thee time thee'll not get thee money!" That really sums up the highs and lows of this business… It's a love/hate thing: you can hate acting because of what it is and the way it makes you feel sometimes, but you *love* it for exactly the same reasons. It's not an even keel, it's up and down; but I'd rather that than a mundane nine to five.'

Bearing in mind how eager viewers were to find out what the future held for Sam Tyler – Dean's mates included – what did they think of the enigmatic ending to the first series?

'People love happy endings,' answers Marshall. 'Happily ever after… I think they

should go against the grain sometimes and keep people hanging, I'd be happy for it to be left on a complete cliff-hanger, you know. Just leave it…'

'What?' asks Dean, 'so you never know what happens to Sam?'

'Yeah, I'd be quite happy to leave it like that.'

Dean's not quite so convinced. Maybe his mates will beat him up if they never get a resolution. 'It is a weird thing trying to figure out how to end it. Trying to satisfy everyone: critics, audiences, fans – I wouldn't like to do it'

They discuss a few alternatives and decide that maybe they'll pitch them anyway: 'For a ten percent residual,' insists Dean, '*each.*'

One idea is to let Chris and Ray take centre stage. 'We could have an accident in 1973 and go back to 1926…' suggests Dean.

'Yeah…' Marshall's got it now. 'Wake up back in time, get hit by another car and end up as Musketeers!'

'…Wake up next to the Horse and Cart then get hit over the head and…'

Wake up as cavemen?

'Why not?'

Why not, indeed…

> **"One minute I'm sat there with Sir Michael Gambon, Joan Collins, Michael Parkinson … then the very next night I'm doing three half-hour sets at a club in Rotherham"**

# DC RAY CARLING

*Jesus*!' Adams twitched in his seat and involuntarily lashed out with his sore foot. Desk Sergeant WPC Phyllis Dobbs ducked back quickly.

'Be careful, you soft wassock! You nearly had me head off.'

'Be careful yourself; you're supposed to be making it better, not worse.'

Phyllis stopped curling the bandage around his slightly swollen foot and gave a cold smile. She gave the bandage a sharp tug, squeezing the foot hard. Adams gave a loud scream and growled under his breath.

'Well … *that's* a noise that brings back happy memories.' DC Ray Carling was stood in the doorway. 'He'll tell you everything you need to know right about now.'

'Morning, Detective,' Thompson said cheerily, 'thanks for popping in. Grab a seat.'

Carling strolled in with a slight swagger.

Phyllis tied the bandage off and left them to it, giving Carling a scathing look as she went. He gave a pantomime shiver as she passed.

'Did someone leave a window open or did that battleaxe just open her legs?' he chuckled once she'd gone. 'Mouth like a sewer, fanny like a bear trap, see it a mile off, can't you?'

*Not that brave then*, Thompson thought, *otherwise he'd have said that to her face*. A certain mathematical ratio regarding the relationship between mouth and trousers popped into his head.

'How'd you do that?' Carling asked, nodding towards Adams's foot and fishing a fag out of his blazer pocket.

'Argument with a chair. Don't worry about it.' There was a pause.

'Thank you for agreeing to talk to us,' Thompson began.

'Not like I had a choice,' grumbled Carling, flicking his fag ash on the floor. 'What do you want to know?'

'Well, we're doing a book and we want to capture the essence of day to day life in the world of urban policing. The highs and lows, the reasons and motivations behind what you do, how you deal with the psychological strain of your occupation…'

Carling looked at Thompson for a moment and then turned to Adams, 'Is he on summat?'

'Other than his high horse? He's asking how you feel about your job.'

'Oh … right,' Carling scratched at his moustache, 'Well. You do what you have to do don't you? If some slag's been a naughty boy then it's our job to slap him down. That's who we are.'

'And you do whatever it takes?' queried Thompson.

Carling leaned forward in his seat. 'If I'm knocking on your door, chances are you've done something to bring me there. I don't give a toss for their arguments or whingeing; if they don't like to play rough they should have kept their noses clean.'

'The end will always justify the means?'

'If it gets some bastard off the streets that should never have been on 'em in the first place, then yeah… As I said, you do what you have to do.'

Carling leaned back again but the look in his eyes showed he was far from relaxed. Thompson ruffled his notes slightly, feeling absurdly nervous all of a sudden.

Adams got to his feet, quickly but carefully. 'Bloody right! I'm sick of all those pansy liberals moaning on about fair treatment and "softly softly".'

Carling smiled, 'You've got it. You want a job like this done you've got to get your hands dirty.'

'Yeah.' Adams lit a cigarette of his own and limped across the room, 'And if some little prick stands between you and a conviction…?'

'You should have the power to knock some sense into him, yeah.'

Adams turned to Carling, pointing with his

cigarette, 'And if you push a little hard and someone gets hurt, then … who cares?'

'Shit happens. Nobody's going to shed a tear for the scum that walks in here. Roll 'em over and move onto the next; you've got the idea.'

A few seconds passed. Nobody said anything.

'Erm…' Thompson shifted in his seat, 'Thanks for coming in. Really appreciate it.'

'Is that it?' asked Carling, getting to his feet.

'That's fine for now, thanks.'

'Oh, right… I'll get on then.' He moved to the door.

'Mind how you go.' Adams said, not looking in his direction.

'Don't worry about me,' Carling smiled, stepping out of the door, 'I know what I'm doing.'

The door closed and Adams sighed.

'Yes…' he said. 'I'm rather afraid you do.'

"If I'm knocking on your door chances are you've done something to bring me there"

# WHATEVER HAPPENED TO ALL THE CLASSY BIRDS?

## An interview with Noreen Kershaw

It's all too easy, immersed in seventies values, the lack of political correctness and the subordination of women in the workplace, to forget the exception that proves the rule: Sergeant Phyllis Dobbs – a woman who could charitably be classed as coming from the 'Battleaxe' School of Femininity. It speaks volumes for the character – and frankly the woman who plays her – that she's the only person who can repeatedly stand up to Gene Hunt (and, on occasion, utter lines far filthier too). Phyllis doesn't suffer fools. She stands no nonsense and speaks her mind. She knows what's what – and what goes on at the station – and what's more, we get the impression that Gene Hunt knows it. Certainly, underneath all the bluster and the insults, he regards Phyllis with a wary respect.

'She's a woman ahead of her time,' laughs

> **"She's a woman ahead of her time... I love it when I get the scripts; some of Phyllis's lines are killers!"**

Noreen Kershaw. 'I love it when I get the scripts; some of Phyllis's lines are killers!'

Noreen knows a good script when she sees one. She was the first Shirley Valentine for Willy Russell when his play debuted in Liverpool in 1986, playing the part for the entirety of its run, bar the famous few performances where Russell himself covered for her when she was ill; and she has two credits with the much-lauded screenwriter Alan Bleasdale – *Boys From the Blackstuff* and *G.B.H.*

She has also worked for some years as a director, having cut her teeth on several episodes of *Coronation Street*. What led her to explore the other side of the camera?

'One job feeds into the other, doesn't it?' she reflects. 'I got interested in telling the whole story, or maybe I'm just a control freak! I really like the process of telling stories, and I wanted to carry that further.'

Having occupied the director's chair and overseen the whole of the business of filming, does she find it difficult to relinquish control when she's working as an actor?

'No,' she says, firmly. 'When I'm acting then that's the hat I'm wearing that day. Although I might try and nick any good ideas,' she laughs, 'and use them later down the line.' In fact, experiencing both sides of the coin, far from making

her want to be involved with the directing when she's acting, has given her a heightened degree of sympathetic insight. 'It's made me very supportive of directors of course; I know what it's like.'

Directing gives her another advantage, too. Since it has become her main pursuit, it's enabled her to be selective about her acting roles. With a second professional string to her bow, she can choose to go after the parts she really wants – *Life On Mars* being one of them.

'I was lucky,' she says. 'I wasn't able to go to the first interview because I had the 'flu, but Claire [Parker, the producer] said they wouldn't cast Phyllis until they'd seen me. I was made up, because it was such a good script that I was desperate to do it. It's a part that any actor would love to play.'

Even if it does mean that people shrink away from her in fear when they bump into her on the street?

'Definitely,' she affirms. 'It's great playing a battleaxe. I'd love to play *really* bad someday … You don't worry about whether people "like" you or not. In real life,' she insists, 'I'm a big sweetheart!'

That's true, and besides, who couldn't love Phyllis, really? As long as you stay on the right side of her.

> **"It's great playing a battleaxe. I'd love to play really bad someday... You don't worry about whether people "like" you or not. In real life, I'm a big sweetheart!"**

'Precisely!' Noreen agrees. 'It was just a perfect part; it's such a good story, such a great idea…'

Two things that are always good news for any actor *or* director.

'Absolutely. That's where the power should lie: in great writing and brave ideas. Stories that reflect our lives and the way we live them. Sometimes,' she reflects, 'it seems that the "suits" in broadcasting get a winning formula and run it to death. But all that's changing now because we're becoming fed up with the same tired formats and faces. People want new and interesting stories and different ways of telling them. There are producers out there whose work is writer-led, and it shows. We have multiple choices – *Life On Mars*, *Shameless*, *Doctor Who*, *The Street* in one year alone – we don't have to watch the "same-old same-old".'

For a moment it feels as if Phyllis herself had walked in.

Noreen laughs again. 'Rant over!'

How, in any sane world, could you ever lose this?'

Thompson looked over to where his colleague was balanced precariously on a child's rocking horse. 'Is there any part of you capable of taking this seriously?' he asked with a sigh.

'Probably not. If I've gone mental, I may as well enjoy it.' Adams stopped rocking. 'None of this is serious, none of this is even real. Can't be. So if I'm going to imagine a world, I may as well have fun with it.'

'Has it occurred to you that we can't *both* be imagining the same thing?'

Adams started rocking again. 'Yes, obviously, but I know my own head when I'm dreaming in it.'

WPC Annie Cartwright walked in. 'Right' Adams continued, 'I'll prove it.'

He got off the toy horse and walked up to her, foolish grin on his face. 'Afternoon officer. Get your kit off!'

Cartwright slapped him hard across the face. 'I may have to put up with that sort of that sort of thing out there, but I don't have to hear it from you.'

Adams stroked his cheek and looked over towards Thompson. 'Fair enough…' he mumbled, '…sorry.'

Cartwright sat down on the empty chair in front of the desk and gave Thompson a forced smile. 'So,' she said, 'what do you want to know?'

'You've answered my main question, really,' Thompson replied, 'as to whether you find the behaviour of your male colleagues hard to deal with.'

'You have no idea.' She sighed. 'It's not the suggestive comments so much…'

'Could've bloody fooled me.' Adams muttered, sitting down a safe distance from the desk. Cartwright stared at him and he dipped his head bashfully.

'… It's more the fact that nobody cares whether you have an opinion or not, whether you might

my mouth shut, despite the fact that I know damn well they're making stupid mistakes.'

'Why don't you just tell them?' Thompson asked.

Cartwright looked at him, 'If you have to ask, you haven't the first idea what it's like.'

'Why do it, then?' Adams asked, 'You must have known what it would be like working here, so why become a policewoman?'

Cartwright smiled. 'Because working bar pumps is no kind of life. And you live in hope, don't you?'

'You could have chosen a different career, though,' Thompson shuffled through the notes in front of him, 'you've got a degree in Psychology, after all.'

'Which means I understand why women get treated the way they do, however much I dislike it.'

She looked back over her shoulder at the hustle and bustle of uniforms and suits beyond the frosted glass window of the door.

'Besides,' she continued, 'things change… the only way I could have got through the door to this place thirty years ago would have been to kill someone.' She smiled at Thompson, 'Now you just have to pass an exam. Give it time and a woman will be running the station. Just hope I'm still around to see it.'

She stood up, 'I've got work to do,' she glanced at Adams, 'y'know, darning, cooking, cleaning … the usual.' She opened the door and stepped out into the corridor before turning back slightly. 'Are you interviewing Hunt later?'

'Of course,' Thompson answered.

'Good… Give him hell!'

She flashed them her biggest smile yet and closed the door.

'Okay,' Adams sighed, 'maybe this isn't my dream after all.'

Thompson tidied his notes and smiled.

'Another slap like that,' he said, 'and I might start believing it's mine.'

" Besides, things change... the only way I could have got through the door to this place thirty years ago would have been to kill someone.... Now you just have to pass an exam... "

# PROPER LITTLE CID GIRL
## An interview with Liz White

Liz is a dedicated professional who endeavours to be as clear and genuine in her responses as possible, not only because she does not want to be misinterpreted – although there's an element of that ('You don't want to come across as a tit,' she says. 'You can't look someone in the eye when it's written down and you seem completely different from how you really are.') – but because she loves acting and takes the business of it seriously, while still retaining an earthy sense of humour.

What were her first impressions of *Life On Mars* when it was offered to her?

'I looked at the first few pages before Sam goes back to 1973 and thought it was quite a pedestrian cop series initially, I didn't think it was anything special. When they made the leap back in time, though … even reading it you could visualise it so strongly. I thought that was stunning, and you latch on really quickly to the idea. I thought it was brilliant. It was the first script I'd read in a long time that was offering something different. When you get a script to read, it's unusual not to recognize the formula straightaway. I saw in a recent *Broadcast* magazine that networks are losing ratings because too many of their dramas are so sanitised and clean-cut; they have such low expectations of what audiences can deal with or understand.'

And audiences are asked to deal with plenty in *Life On Mars*, embracing as it does cop series, thriller, comedy, nostalgia trip, drama…with a mind-expanding twist and no fear of throwing some weightier subjects into the mix, such as the blatant sexism meted out to Annie Cartwright.

'It's got to be portrayed: it was a massive part of being a woman in the seventies, it was a very sexist world. That's why it's great being a woman now, because a lot of the work's been done. There's still inequality – which men suffer from as well – but a lot of the hard work was done in the sixties and seventies, although it was still fairly rocky, particularly in the male-dominated world of the police force. You forget, because we've got it comparatively easy these days, but living through that … those *remarks*. I'm the youngest in my family, with two older brothers, and it was just like being five again. You get told off for answering back too much and you soon learn that it's easier to stay quiet… or you risk being brave, you try and change your life by fighting back. That's what it feels like being in Annie's shoes, like being a little sister again, understanding when

to keep your mouth shut and when it's your turn to stand up for yourself. I'd never really paid it that much attention: growing up in the nineties it's easy to forget, so doing this was a vivid reminder of what it must have been like.

'It's hard sometimes because I get so involved playing her; I can feel her frustration starting to brew and what's in the script doesn't always match what *I'd* like to say to Gene! There have been episodes where things have been said and she's been a witness to them – not necessarily things directed at her, or even an issue to do with sexual politics – but a way of going about things that isn't right, or isn't the best way to achieve results. But then her knowledge as a person isn't even considered, because she's a woman.'

Are there times when Liz hankers for Annie to take on a streak of Noreen Kershaw's Phyllis – the loud-mouthed battleaxe desk sergeant?

'It's just not part of her personality,' she demurs. 'But then, if Annie had a personality like Phyllis she probably wouldn't get anywhere – except into Phyllis's job perhaps – because she'd be more trouble than she's worth to people like

**"It was just like being five again. You get told off for answering back too much and you soon learn that it's easier to stay quiet... or you risk being brave, you try and change your life by fighting back. That's what it feels like being in Annie's shoes"**

Gene. It's because she can do her job quietly, be very efficient and useful, that she gets to be involved in the police work at all. If she was more assertive they'd never let her near it."

And Annie does have skills of her own which are called upon occasionally, such as her psychology degree. Is that something Liz would like to make more of?

'Of course,' she says. 'But again there's that need to keep quiet. And having said that, we've all done degrees and forgotten them: I did A-Level sociology, Marxism and the rest but I'd struggle to tell you any precise theories now…

'Obviously, as an actor you want to do more, you want an objective to the scene so that you can play it, which is harder to do when you've only got a few lines. But *Life On Mars* will always be Sam Tyler's story, and that can't be

say, "what are we going to do with you?" I don't mind that she doesn't believe him, but I want her to do something like take him to hospital, get him some treatment, some advice. Take some sort of positive action rather than simply go on a date. Perhaps she's using diversionary tactics…'

Maybe she just fancies Sam too much to have him sectioned?

'Yeah – "He's mad but he's got a nice bum!"'

The feeling must be reciprocated: all blokes like a girl in uniform after all.

Liz is less than convinced. 'It's horrible! The costume is really restrictive, the hair too, it's like a bird's nest; I look like Margaret Thatcher! It's a pain, but it does help you get into character. Sometimes I think I'm not glamorous enough for a lead in this kind of show … although I do like the fact that Annie's not a dolly bird, she's just a normal northern woman.'

As well as television Liz has appeared in film – including Mike Leigh's multiple award-winning *Vera Drake* – and in the theatre, where she was part of a collective who won a coveted Samuel Beckett Award for their work. Does she prefer one medium over the others?

'I like them all,' she says. 'they're all acting… The writing's always the most important thing, though. If you get a good script it doesn't matter what medium you're in.'

forgotten. When you get a script you look at what function your character has in the piece, what narrative device you're fulfilling, that's always the best way of looking at it.'

What role, in her view, does Annie fulfil? 'The moral compass of the scene,' she laughs, 'which means you're there to nod at the audience now and then when someone does something naughty.'

There's no doubt that Sam's life would be a lot worse were Annie not around, since she seems the only one to whom he can talk about his 'visions'. Does Annie believe a word of it, though?

Liz considers. 'No, I don't think she believes him, although she does think that he's got a serious problem – which he has. But every episode he comes to her and tells her that he shouldn't be here, he's from another time, and all she does is shake her head and

> **"I don't mind that she doesn't believe him, but I want her to do something like take him to hospital, get him some treatment... Take some sort of positive action rather than simply go on a date!"**

## TX SCRIPT EXTRACT - Episode One

**INT. POLICE STATION - SIDE ROOM - DAY**

*WPC ANNIE CARTWRIGHT twists SAM'S head to the other side. His neck makes a loud cracking noise. ANNIE is late 20's with a face that lets you know there's a good mind whirring away.*

**ANNIE:** Do you feel like you're gonna heave up?

**SAM:** I feel a bit nauseous.

*She walks over to tidy away the First Aid kit.*

**ANNIE:** You'll do. You've had hangovers worse.

**SAM:** Are you a doctor?

**ANNIE:** I'm about as qualified as Dr Kildare. I'm part of the Women's Department.

**SAM:** What?

*But SAM doesn't move. He just sits there starring at her. She stares back.*

**ANNIE:** Don't they have plonks in Hyde? Go on sir, off you jolly well trot. What now?

**SAM:** What's your name?

**ANNIE:** WPC Cartwright.

**SAM:** No, first name?

**ANNIE:** Annie.

**SAM:** I was four in 1973 Annie.

*She looks at him, confused.*

**Sam:** Hit me.

**ANNIE:** Don't tempt me.

*But he isn't and she can see it. He goes towards her.*

**SAM:** Go on.

**ANNIE:** You've been in an accident.

**SAM:** Hit me.

*But she won't. He gives up and turns away. She suddenly punches him in the kidneys.*

**SAM:** Argh! Shit!

*She grabs him from behind. Just then GENE throws open the door - clocks SAM bent double.*

**ANNIE:** (O.O.V) I'm sorry sir.

**GENE:** Hey, hey. Good girl, prostate probe and no jelly.

## CHARACTER LIFE

Many actors often build up their character's back story beyond what is written in the script. Whilst not necessarily part of the official character's biography, it can often help shape an actor's portrayal and reactions to events in the story.

When talking with Matthew Graham, it was clear that Liz White had taken some time and thought over Annie's home life. 'It's always interesting,' Matthew reflects, 'when actors want to take their characters home [in an episode]. It shows they're thinking about their character's motivation and reasons for making certain decisions.' In Liz's head, when Annie is not at work, she spends time caring for her invalid father, who is an ex-policeman. Annie's desires and aspirations are based around making her father proud; so that even though he can no longer serve in the force, there is a part of him still solving crimes and righting wrongs.

# DCI GENE HUNT

They'd been on their own now for an hour, pacing the narrow aisles of the broken and discarded.

'You reckon they've forgotten about us?' Thompson asked, flicking through a battered suitcase of projector slides.

'Nah,' Adams kicked at the dust balls at his feet. 'Just showing us who's boss, aren't they? Making us hang about a bit.'

Thompson raised his eyebrow at the contortions in evidence on the slide he was looking at, 'I'm amazed this hasn't been pocketed for someone's private collection; it's certainly "specialist" enough.'

The sound of a siren was sudden enough to make him drop the slide. The dark room was strobe-lit by blue emergency flashes, the air filled with shouting.

'Don't tell me they've put an alarm on 'em?' Adams dashed for the door, hoping to stop the panic. It was locked, closed solid.

'What's happening?' Thompson had to shout to be heard now.

There was the crackle of police radios, the squeal of metal, the song of ambulance sirens…

Adams looked back towards Thompson, who seemed to have slumped unconscious to the ground. Lit by a spotlight, the roar of rotor blades and a wind that sent objects flying from the shelves surrounded his prone body.

'*Gently!*' a voice shouted. '*Take it slow!*'

'This can't be real,' Adams whispered, as Thompson began to rise from the floor, airlifted from the past by a future neither of them could see.

'*Pull out!*' the stranger's voice shouted, '*there's nobody else here.*'

'Wait!' Adams shouted, 'what about me?'

He ran into the middle of the room, waving his arms in the glare of the spotlight. 'What about me? I'm still here! Don't leave me!'

'Alright.'

The room was normal again. Gene Hunt stood in the open doorway. 'Come 'ere and you can 'ave a quick hug, then daddy's got to get back to work, okay?'

Adams looked around. Thompson was sat down behind his desk, a dazed look in his eyes.

'You fairies need a little time on your own?' Gene asked.

'Sorry,' Adams mumbled, red in the face, 'just working on a bit of the book, y'know, role-play sort of thing.'

'Obviously. I'm just glad you hadn't got to the pillow-biting chapter.'

'Erm … thank you for coming in.' Thompson had slowly got a grip. 'If you could just take a seat, there are a few questions we'd like to ask.'

'That's not quite what I had in mind,' Hunt announced. 'I'm a busy man and I haven't got the time for the likes of you two so,' he pointed at Adams, '*you* sit down; both of you shut up, pick up your pencils and take a bit of dictation.'

Adams sat down, only realising he'd done as he was told a few seconds later, by then incapable of arguing about it as Hunt was in full flow.

'Chapter One, Page One: A Day In The Life of DCI Gene Hunt. Clever old Gene strolls in about mid-morning, has a cup of tea – maybe even a bacon and egg butty, yolk runny, bacon crisp – opens up his case file, catches a few silly bastards who're up to no good in his city, gives 'em what for, bangs 'em up and gets to The Railway Arms in time for several pints with a whisky chaser and a couple of hands of cards. Gene then goes to sleep. End of chapter. Any questions?'

Thompson and Adams looked at each other; Thompson slowly stuck his hand up.

'No time for questions.' Hunt smiled, 'I do what I do and get the job done. There's no book here, no juicy story, no controversy, no time for stupid ponces like you two getting under my feet and stopping me

being where I need to be: on the street and on the job. And if I find out that either of you have been poking around where you've no business in the lives of me or my men you'd better watch out. Because you'll wake up one night to find the Gene Genie singing you a lullaby, with a hipflask in his gob and a sock full of gravel in his hand. I don't take kindly to people nosing around, especially those who force their way in here with pieces of paper and high and bloody mighty attitudes. Do you understand?'

Adams and Thompson nodded.

'Good. That said, pleased to meet you. Make yourselves at home and the drinks are on you, later.'

Thompson put his hand up again.

'Piss off.' Hunt smiled, sweet as you like, and walked out.

Adams turned to Thompson, they looked at each other for a few seconds.

'Well,' said Thompson eventually, 'that was informative.'

# TRUST THE GENE GENIE
## An interview with Philip Glenister

There is an understandable caution to interviewing the man who plays DCI Gene Hunt: he has, after all, demonstrated his own none-too-subtle interrogation technique several times on screen. Thankfully Philip Glenister shares none of the belligerence of the role he plays. In fact it takes very little persuasion to make him confess…

'I first heard about *Life On Mars* through my agent and, when she described it to me, I thought it sounded crazy, utterly *utterly* ridiculous: I had to read it! As Kudos were behind it you could predict it was going to be a bit different: I knew that from *Spooks* and *Hustle*; they're a very slick outfit. So I was intrigued, really, because of a whole mixture of things. Once I'd started reading I couldn't put it down. I loved it, I loved the character…the things he said made me laugh out loud in places. It was one of those rare moments for an actor where I knew immediately what this character should be like; it just came off the page … I could picture his *clothes*, the way he spoke … I had an acting revelation moment!'

It's not all that surprising of course – who wouldn't want to play Gene Hunt? – but, as if that weren't sufficient to convince him, he also knew that he would be working alongside John Simm again, for the *third* time, as it happened. Was that a factor in his agreeing to take the part?

'My immediate thought was simple: "Oh Christ, Do I have to work with John Simm again?" He laughs. 'No…I'm a huge fan of John's work as an actor. I'd worked with him on both *Clocking Off* and *State of Play* – *Clocking Off* was my show, *State of Play* was his. We'd guested in each other's shows, and this time we got to do a double act: that was the way we saw it.

'It really wasn't a difficult proposition to say yes to, though, was it? I got to do a seventies cop show! After the first couple of episodes

*Left: Sam and Gene cautiously wait for a sign from hostage-taker Reg Cole in Epsiode Six.*

*Above right: Always protective of his team, Gene offers Sam a 'subtle' warning about his internal investigation in Episode Seven.*

came out, mates were ringing me up, saying: 'I have to be in this show!' Everybody wanted a slice of it.'

It must have felt particularly satisfying, to be involved in a show that engendered that sort of reaction.

'Of course,' he agrees. But you have to be careful not to have your head turned by that sort of thing. Even when we were shooting there were emails coming through from the people at Kudos who were watching the footage we'd done and they were saying how good it was all looking, how wonderful it was. John and I took it with a pinch of salt because there's no way your producer's going to come back to you and say the rushes look awful. There's always that worry when something's been built up so big, because ultimately, the audience is going to judge you. So it was exciting, but there was a lot of nervousness – what if this really does *bomb*? It's always best to keep a level head about these things until it's out and an audience has seen it and digested it. Then you get the second series and have to go through it all again!'

With greater expectations than before?

'Oh, yes…'

And with his 'sex symbol' status fully established, of course…

He laughs again. 'Rubbish!'

They love him though, the ladies… even the

> **"I thought it sounded crazy, utterly *utterly* ridiculous: I had to read it!"**

vaguest of internet browsing will reveal how much they adore the Gene Genie.

'Where are they all?' he protests. 'They haven't exactly been throwing themselves at me in the streets! Until that happens, I don't believe a word of it.'

The fan reaction surprised him, though. A lot of those who write to him about *Life On Mars* are teenagers, 'which seems weird. You can imagine them writing to Ant and Dec or David Beckham or someone like that, but me?' He wonders whether their interest was sparked by their mums and dads having grown up in the seventies: kids catching on to their parents nostalgia. Mind you, he reckons, 'I wouldn't have been interested in my parents' childhood! The early fifties, dark and depressing, rock and roll hadn't even really kicked off…

'That's the good thing about choosing the seventies as an era,' he concludes. 'It has a wider appeal: since the late sixties, the birth of the teenager, when popular culture meshed itself onto society, there's much more of a bond

between generations now; we can empathise with one another more...'

Certainly there's widespread interest in the seventies. The music has gained itself a whole new audience, from prog rock to singer-songwriters – punk will be next. And seventies-influenced fashion can be seen on any street – not that Gene Hunt's seminal seventies' garb is likely to feature on the catwalks any time soon.

'I'd worked with costume designer Emma Rosenthal on *Clocking Off* and she's great, she does her homework, a real stickler for detail. She phoned me beforehand and asked if I had any thoughts, so I told her to think seventies football manager, which she loved. When I went in for the fitting there was the camel coat, there were the shoes...'

Ah yes, those shoes.

'Look,' says Glenister, 'they're going to get a show of their own, they've got a separate contract stipulating a close-up every other shot. BBC3, this autumn, watch out for

it...'

But will they cross the Atlantic to feature in the American version of *Life On Mars*, produced by David E. Kelly of *Boston Legal* and *Ally McBeal* fame?

'They'll be starring,' he affirms.

How did he feel about the making of the transatlantic version?

'It is weird,' he concedes. 'Someone else playing my part... When I was over there to publicise the run of the show on BBC America I was asked who I would cast as Hunt. "*Me*," I told them, "with David Hasselhoff as Sam." I thought they should set it in San Francisco; Gene should be the old-school Karl Malden type and Sam should be gay. Gay cop and very *very* straight cop. There was a very long silence when I suggested that!'

Commuting to San Francisco, though, would be tough.

'It was bad enough filming in Manchester; travelling up Sunday night, coming back late

> **"Look, those shoes are going to get a show of their own, they've got a separate contract stipulating a close-up every other shot. BBC3, this autumn, watch out for it..."**

Friday. It was harder for my other half than it was for me of course: having a young family, she's the one who had to put her career on hold while I was buggering about in a seventies costume. I had to play it down sometimes. Not sound as if I was enjoying myself too much. "Oh … stuck in the studio, love … Nah, no screeching around corners in the Cortina today."'

Driving the car was something he obviously enjoyed a great deal.

'Oh yes. Doing a few stunts, learning my handbrake turns, that was great fun. I couldn't do all of it though; either because the insurance people wouldn't let me or because of the lack of time – some of the car scenes would be shot by a second unit while we got on with scenes where you could see my face.'

Phil has an impressive list of credits to his name, from classics like *Vanity Fair* to historical adventure such as *Hornblower* to contemporary crime drama *The Vice*. Does he have a favourite acting medium?

'Voiceovers! Radio! You can turn up looking like crap and you don't have to learn your lines! But I'm most comfortable with film and television. I used to do a lot of stage work but I'm one of those people who gets easily bored

with repetition, I'm afraid. I love the rehearsal process, those three or four weeks when you get to dissect a play, get it all wrong and then, *eventually*, get it right – that's exciting. Then you've got your opening night and you're sick as a pig with nerves … Then you're waiting for the reviews, and if you're lucky you've got a hit show … *Then* I get bored. Especially if it's a long run, and it's a real slog in the West End; eight shows … matinees … when I become king of Equity I'm going to ban all matinees!'

And were there any experiences from filming *Life On Mars* which he would rather not repeat?

'Filming in an abattoir for Episode Four; hearing the sound of animals waiting to be slaughtered. John and I didn't eat meat for about two days after that. I couldn't walk past a butcher's without weeping!

'Wearing Speedos in Episode Two was *very* embarrassing. There are times that you look at yourself in this business and wonder what the hell you're doing! Middle of April, freezing your rocks off in nothing but Speedo trunks, sprinting along a canal path pretending to be a seventies copper. At the age of forty-three, I ask you, where did it all go wrong?'

*Opposite: Top left: A contemplative Gene weighs up Sam's 'gay boy science' alongside his more physical approach*
*Opposite: Top right: It's not all hard work though, as laughs are often had on set*
*Opposite: Lower right: The Gene-Genie springs in to action.*

*Right: To get the best action shots of Gene driving (and Sam's reactions), the Cortina is often strapped up with multiple cameras, which can make navigating a problem!*

# SPEAKING LIKE A COMPLETE HUNT

You can say what you like about DCI Gene Hunt – as long as he doesn't hear you – but you could never accuse him of mincing his words. There can be little doubt that his turn of phrase didn't get him to the rank he's achieved, since he is to smooth talking what a cheese-grater is to a mink coat dipped in oil. Nonetheless his straight-talking manner does give us some memorable quotes and verbal gems to admire, cringe at or – if we think for one moment we can get away with it – re-use in the social situations of our choosing.

From the moment we meet him – waking to a hangover with all the grace of a buffalo with thrush – we know the kind of man he is. Punching Sam in the gut and then holding him up by his lapels, it's abundantly clear that winning friends and influencing people is not high on Gene's agenda.

> **Gene:** They reckon you've got concussion, but I don't give a tart's furry cup if half your brains are falling out. Don't ever waltz into my kingdom acting like you're king of the jungle.
> **Sam:** Who the hell are you?
> **Gene:** Gene Hunt. Your DCI. And it s 1973. Almost dinner time. I'm 'avin 'oops.

Still, he is only too happy to share his thoughts on aspects of policing. On the importance of good relations with the youth of the day:

*'Anything happens to this motor and I come over your houses and stamp on all your toys, got it?'* (the kids nod) *'Good kids.'* EPISODE ONE

On the criminal element:

*'[He's] an unpleasant little scrotum, what we in the business call a necessary evil.'* EPISODE FOUR

On the contentious subject of planting evidence:

*'I've never fitted anyone up who didn't deserve it.'* EPISODE TWO

Or the benefits of caution when dealing with armed criminals:

*'Drop your weapons! You are surrounded by armed bastards!'* EPISODE THREE

He is happy to offer a sympathetic ear, and has consistently proved his sensitivity on awkward subjects such as religion or sexuality:

*'I'm not a Catholic myself…but isn't there something about "Thou shalt not suck off rent boys?"'* EPISODE FOUR

He is particularly good with the female officers on his team, stopping WPC Annie Cartwright from following him up the stairs in The Warren nightclub with the injunction:

*'VIP lounge, love. I don't think that includes off-duty slags with glitter in their hair, do you?* EPSIODE FOUR

And he is clearly in touch with his feminine side when it comes to the gentler pursuits, such as cookery:

**Gene** (after Sam has despaired of the ingredients with which he is supposed to run a pub kitchen): *'So, what do you want?'*

**Sam:** *'Olive oil would be nice, bit of coriander…'* (Gene stares at him) *'It's a herb.'*

**Gene:** *'Well this is Trafford Park. You've got more chance of finding an ostrich with a plum up its arse.'* EPISODE FIVE

Perhaps this is what makes him attractive to women…

*'She wants me. Poor bitch.'* EPISODE SIX

> Phyllis: I'm knackered.
> Gene: Serves you right for staying up ruttin' all night with that new fella of yours. Do you let his guide dog watch?
> Phyllis: His guide dog's giving your Mam one-from behind. (Gene looks shocked)
> Gene: Whatever happened to all the classy birds?

At least we can always say that he is a man who is thoroughly in touch with himself.

**Gene:** *'I think you've forgotten who you're talking to.'*

**Sam:** *'An overweight, over the hill, nicotine-stained, borderline alcoholic homophobe with a superiority complex and an unhealthy obsession with male bonding.'*

**Gene:** *'You make that sound like a bad thing.'* EPISODE EIGHT

# LOST AND FOUND:
# DI SAM TYLER

There was a Gene Hunt-sized hole in the air of the Lost and Found room a full half hour after the man himself had left; that and the lingering atmosphere of a future (or just reality?) briefly tasted.

They were quiet, the writers; sat behind their table. There was an unspoken fear that moving too much within this rarefied atmosphere would bring either a DCI or a phantom helicopter into the room. Neither could say which they would fear the most. Thompson shuffled paper occasionally, more out of the need to be doing something than any practical purpose. Adams smoked cigarettes, one after the other; cigarettes are safe in the short term.

The door opened and DI Sam Tyler walked in. The final interviewee.

They all watched one another; the detective uncomfortable through uncertainty, the writers just as awkward because of what they *did* know. As usual it was Thompson who found his professional feet quickest:

'Sorry, Detective Inspector Tyler, please do take a seat.'

He did so, tucking the Saint Christopher medal he wore into his shirt as it swung out from beneath the collar.

'So,' he asked, 'what do you want to talk about, then?'

And there it lay, the challenge, the *decision*…

'Well,' said Adams. 'That's the thing isn't it? What to talk about? There's the safe or the interesting… and a choice between the two.'

Tyler gave a half smile, slightly dismissive, 'Don't know what you mean.'

Adams leaned forward. '*I know where you're from*.'

A slight twitch in Tyler's left eye, 'I'm sure it's in the file, yeah…'

Adams shook his head. 'No, I mean *really*.'

They stared at one another. Thompson shifted in his seat, uncertain whether his colleague was really about to go through with it, uncertain also as to how he felt about it.

Adams had already made his decision: 'As in, from the future…'

There was one hell of a pause.

Then Tyler jumped at Adams, hands aiming for his throat, the momentum sending the chair he sat on tumbling back so that both men went flying.

Thompson fell back himself, moving out of harm's way and overcompensating so that he also lost his balance and ended up on the floor. The two brawling men landed on his outstretched legs making him cry out.

'Wake me up!' Tyler shouted. 'Wake me up!'

Which was a predictable enough response after all – not that hindsight is a particularly useful thing at any juncture, least of all while being choked by a man who has just stopped giving up on getting home.

*'Wake me up!'*

Adams tried to force his fingers between Tyler's, open up the man's grip for a little air.

The room was becoming … *vague* around them.

He could hear the sound of an ECG machine, beeping faster as the heart rate it monitored quickened its pace. Was that him? Was that his heart? Doctors shouted. Nurses came running.

Tyler's face crumpled; he could hear them too. Maybe the heart was his then…

*'Wake me up!'*

The helicopter was back; the chopping of air by rotor blades.

Metal was squealing again.

(And all the while the sound of hospital machinery and the fuss of medics…)

Lost and Found had all too many futures fighting for attention. Dream layered on dream, reality on reality.

'Sam!' a voice shouted – both policeman and writer looking around for where it came from. 'DI Tyler! I'm sorry, DI Tyler; there's been some sort of mistake.'

The grip on Adams throat started to loosen, Tyler becoming distracted by the voice.

'We know you're not really from the future, that would be ridiculous … just a rumour we'd heard from some of the constables … apparently you said something about it when you first arrived here … it wasn't meant to be serious … DI Tyler?'

The voice was Thompson, trying to back-pedal as fast as his mind would let him.

'We didn't mean any offence… Sorry. Just a joke…'

The helicopter was fading – flying off through the years – the heart monitor was slowing.

Lost…

…and *found*.

Tyler let go of Adams' throat.

'Sorry,' he mumbled, distracted, disorientated…

'Don't mention it,' Adams croaked.

They looked towards Thompson.

'Well now,' he said, nudging his glasses back up his nose, 'looks like we've started off on the wrong foot, doesn't it, rather?  What say you get off my legs and we start afresh; maybe over a nice pint?'

# MY PROBLEM WOULD ROCK YOUR WORLD

### An interview with John Simm

John Simm surely has one of the toughest jobs on *Life On Mars*. Not just because of his workload – although the filming schedules have been harsh and most certainly took their toll – but by the simple fact that *Life On Mars* rests so heavily on its leading man. The show is unusual in that the main character is in *every* scene, which makes for long days and an almost unprecedented need to ensure the actor representing that focal point of the show *gets it right*.

Not that there was ever the least doubt that he would be up to the task. As director Bharat Nalluri has commented elsewhere in this book, while he may not be a conventional 'square-jawed' hero there are few actors working in British television today who can be relied on to give so believable a performance. Besides, Sam Tyler is hardly your usual hero. Matthew Graham memorably introduced him in a script note for Episode One as: 'If Sam were a colour, he'd be spearmint.' John's initial assessment was equally candid: 'When you first see him, in 2006, he isn't particularly likeable; he's quite pedantic and anal, and he doesn't seem to have much of a sense of humour.' Of course, what draws audiences to the character – and what makes him increasingly sympathetic as he struggles to come to terms

> **"I usually take parts that are based in reality so, when I read the script, I thought that if I could make it believable – make it real – to *myself*, then that would be the real challenge"**

**Left:** *Sam learns that his type of policing differs wildly to that of 1973.*

**Above:** *We take Sam's journey alongside him; we see his confusion, anger and pain across the entire series.*

with his situation – is Sam's emotional response to the crazy circumstances he finds himself in. John was very much drawn to the concept.

'I usually take parts that are based in reality so, when I read the script, I thought that if I could make it believable – make it real – to *myself*, then that would be the real challenge, because it's such an outlandish, ridiculous idea. Also, it's a big mainstream drama on BBC1 and I'd never really done that, so I was curious to get across to that audience.'

Whether or not his previous work could be defined as 'mainstream', there is no doubting its quality. From a humble start in *Rumpole of the Bailey* and *Heartbeat* he went on to appear in the groundbreaking series *Cracker*, where he gave Robbie Coltrane's freelancing police psychologist Fitz a hard time as a sociopathic young man who would keep killing people he disagreed with. It was his lead role in *Cracker* creator Jimmy McGovern's *The Lakes* (1999) that really brought him to the public's attention however, and a string of rewarding roles followed in film and television including *Human Traffic* (1999), *Clocking Off* (2000) – a show created by Paul Abbott, the writer of Simm's *Cracker* episode – *24 Hour Party People* (2002), *Crime and Punishment* (2002), in which he was a definitive Rashkolnikov, and *State of Play* (2003) – again created by Abbott. In 2004 he starred in *Sex Traffic*, a raw and uncompromising two-parter about the trade in Eastern European women for prostitution, which won no less than eight BAFTAs, four RTS Television Awards and a Prix Italia.

Sam Tyler joins a long list of fictional alter-egos on his CV, but how much of what we see on screen does the actor bring to the role?

'A lot of it really. I had plenty of input [including the suggestion of the medallion Tyler wears throughout the series, a Saint Christopher – the patron saint of travellers]. As an actor you give him the mannerisms,

they don't get written down on a page. With the look of him, I didn't really want to be wearing dodgy suits like everyone else so I thought if it *is* in his head, he'll have a vision of what he thinks is cool in the seventies, and that would go back to what he would have watched on television, like *The Sweeney* or *The Professionals*. He's about my age so I did it from my point of view, and the only person that I could think of from that time who had short hair – which is what Sam arrives with – was Bodie from *The Professionals*. He wore leather jackets so I kept that in the back of my mind, an approximation of it anyway, and the look was more or less based on that.'

He is on record as being somewhat nostalgic about the era itself.

'I was born in 1970 so my personal memories of the seventies are a bit vague. I do remember some of it very clearly: 1977 for some reason – I remember a specific T-shirt that I wore, which had a *Starsky and Hutch* yellow transfer on the front. I remember the Sex Pistols too, and seeing punks. I remember Elvis Presley dying in 1977 really, really vividly. Music does that, brings memories flooding back… And there were some toys I had that I remember very well – I had a Strika bike rather than a Chopper; it was green and I loved it very much.

'It was great to go back and rediscover that era. For the first month at least I was looking at all the magazines on set and I think I read every single one of them about twice. The pictures of footballers, the big Curly Wurlys, Party Sevens and all that.'

Given a chance to go back and revisit a

**"I wouldn't go anywhere near the seventies! I'm seventies'd out, me! I'd pick something entirely different... I'd go to The Cavern and watch The Beatles..."**

period of history, is it one he'd choose? 'Mate, I wouldn't go anywhere near the seventies! I'm seventies'd out, me! So I definitely wouldn't, no. I'd pick something entirely different. There's a few specific things: I'd probably go to Calvary and see if Jesus Christ really did get crucified; I'd go to The Cavern and watch The Beatles; I'd go back and watch Elvis; I'd stand outside the Dakota building and stop Mark Chapman shooting John Lennon… things like that. I'd say if it was anything it'd be the sixties for me.'

As well as having to adjust to seventies fashions, Sam has to weather the treatment he receives from the other detectives at the station. Still, as the series develops the character does find himself becoming more a

***Opposite Top:*** *In Episode Seven, Ray pushes Sam to the limits, flaunting his rule-breaking, teasing and even provoking a fist-fight.*

***Left:*** *Sometimes, Sam's frustration bubbles over into anger, and he becomes more like Gene every time.*

part of the team, as John reflects:

'They rub off on each other, I think. They learn to work together even though they are completely different. Gene's the boss and they've all learnt from him but Sam's methods influence the rest of CID, especially Chris. Sam can't stand Ray, although he likes Chris and he tries his best to teach him stuff; but even Chris thinks he's a little odd. He says [in Episode Eight] 'I don't underestimate you boss, I just don't understand you,' and it's as simple as that. I think they probably all feel like that. Sam has the knowledge of how things are going to turn out and he knows about things like multi-tasking and taping interviews and they do it and they take it on board. His knowledge of the future is his only weapon and the only thing he can work with. And it's quite hard for Gene because he just thinks Sam's a nutter! But Sam learns from Gene too – a little humanity and using his gut instinct. It's a perfect "buddy-buddy" cop thing but with a really weird twist to it.'

As the star of a show with a firmly established 'cult' following, he has entered the domain of the online message board and the fan site. Some actors find that intimidating, some relish the feedback. Is it an aspect of the role that he feels comfortable with?

'I've looked on some of the fan sites and it's very flattering that they love it. But I don't go too deep into it, you can't as an actor really, I just skim it and that's enough.'

It would be surprising if he had the time to do anything else, considering the hours he put in being Sam Tyler. One of the most difficult challenges in a role like this is surely keeping it fresh, maintaining the energy over the long filming period. Does it get to a point when it all starts to blur a little?

'Sometimes! It is such a long, long job for me; I really just get up and go to work, do what I have to do and go home! I enjoy it when it comes out, I enjoy it when I can go home and

forget about it for a while. But this series has been like an endurance test for me, really. It's so full-on. All those months away from home, it's a long time. It was all very well when I was younger and I did *The Lakes* and stuff, because I was free and single, you know?'

John is married to his *24 Hour Party People* co-star Kate McGowan and has a young son, Ryan, something he has been happy to admit informed the way he approached Sam Tyler meeting his own father in the show:

'I think of how I feel about my son – it affects anything to do with kids that I ever do now. I just get an overwhelming feeling and realise it must have been the same for my dad with me and I realise how he must feel about his dad. To get the chance to meet your dad as a young man is a mad thing. Sam is really protective over his dad, he wants to think the best of him even though he left him when he was really young, and he refuses to believe he could be wrong about him.

'It was very strange calling Lee Ingleby "dad" though. He's about five years younger than me so it felt ridiculous!'

With filming for *Life On Mars* concluded, what is he looking forward to doing next?

'Film I'd like … Five or six weeks: it's a different way of working. Or actually I'd like to do nothing and maybe do some voiceovers for a while!'

# LOST AND FOUND:
# THE RAILWAY ARMS

'That'll be thirty-three pence, *mon brave*…' Nelson said, placing three pints of beer in front of Tyler, Adams and Thompson. The accent was pure theatre – he was as Jamaican as the Pope and, however much he could occasionally be heard to wax lyrical about the Kingston sunshine dappling the palm leaves around his Grandmother's front porch, the closest he'd been to the island was a night getting ripped on Bacardi. He smiled, flashing teeth like the penny signs on his till.

'Robbing bastard,' came Gene Hunt's opinion from behind them. 'If you're going to throw that sort of money away, you may as well add another on the bill. Usual for me, Nelson – they are, of course, paying.'

Nelson gave Adams a glance. The writer nodded.

'While you're there…' Ray Carling had just walked in. 'Saves me queuing.'

Thompson looked around. They were the only people at the bar. Carling leaned between them. 'Don't forget Chris, either, will you?' he smiled, without even a hint of sincerity. 'He'll only throw his dolly out the pram otherwise, won't you, Chris?'

'She can't afford the mink coat, Nick, you arse', Chris said to himself, absently pouring a drop more mild into his mouth, eyes glued to *Sale of the Century* on the wood-veneered Thorn television that Tyler had recently fixed to the wall in one corner of the bar.

'Take that as a yes,' Ray winked, and sat down next to Hunt, who was shuffling a deck of cards with all the speed and dexterity of a croupier on a coke binge.

The door opened again and the last few familiar faces from beneath the smoke clouds of the CID office stepped in, one of whom opened his mouth to speak; but the writer beat him to it.

'Drink for everyone,' he sighed, slapping a couple of pound notes down on the counter.

'Look at you, all rich,' Thompson smiled.

'Yeah, made of money, me; I could probably buy the entire place for what we spent on those train tickets…' His smile faded and his eyes went vacant for a second before one of the detectives reaching for his pint jolted his elbow and brought him back to the present.

'Sorry, pal. Thanks for the beer.'

'Don't worry about it.' Adams looked at Thompson. 'We're sinking. You do know that, don't you?'

Thompson grabbed his glass and shook his head. 'Just drink your drink, and don't worry about it.' There was a roar from the corner table where Hunt had just taken his first hand. 'It's bound to be the first of many.'

And it was. A torrent of booze had crossed the bar before the night was over. And when it came to calling 'Time', Nelson reached for the pull that hung from the large brass bell above his till and wasn't altogether surprised to find it missing.

'Thieves and scallywags, old son,' Hunt slurred, the string of the pull clearly hanging from the breast pocket of his jacket. 'Rest assured that I shall not sleep until the bastards are brought to justice.' He threw Nelson a salute and spun on his heels, bringing himself face to face with Adams, who was leaning on the back of a chair to stop himself falling over.

'Ah … the book boy, working on his final chapter.'

'Hardly,' Adams mumbled, taking deep breaths, trying to quell the uncertain bubbling in his stomach.

Hunt gave a broad smile, followed by a broader belch. 'You don't get it, do you? You wanted to know what it was all about, what made us lot tick?' He brought his face down to Adams. 'You're *looking* at it. If you want to know how a copper does what he does, how he gets himself out of bed every morning, how he faces the bloody day with its shit and grind then don't watch him *do* his job…' He gestured around the pub: to Chris practising martial arts moves in front of the telly, Ray trying his luck on a WPC in the corner, Sam laughing with Annie. 'Watch him try and forget what his job bloody *is*.'

He stood up, patted Adams forcefully on the shoulder and walked back over to his card game. Adams subsided slowly under the table, the push from Hunt enough to take the fight out of him.

'I'll make a note of that,' he dribbled, and promptly passed out.

# NELSON'S COLUMN

## An interview with Tony Marshall

There is a precedent of course: the barman who offers not only a welcome ear for our hero's woes but who is also capable of offering up a few wise words to send him on his way. It's a character that's appeared many times in fiction – and probably will again for the simple reason that it works – and, in the case of *Life On Mars*, it's a role filled by actor Tony Marshall. Familiar to TV audiences from his recurring roles in series such as *All Quiet on the Preston Front* or *Only Fools and Horses*, Tony is only too happy to offer Sam a little Jamaican – or, if he's being honest, *Mancunian* – wisdom from time to time. As Nelson – manager of the CID watering hole, the Railway Arms – he's perfectly happy keeping detectives' whistles wetted and bar-tops dry.

'It's absolutely great, isn't it?' he says when asked about *Life On Mars*. 'Quantum Leap was the closest thing I could relate the show to when I read the first script. It's very refreshing, and it comes from the period in the seventies I grew up in. Some of the phrases I hear when we're shooting … it's all very nostalgic!'

He's more than old enough to be drinking, then: what's his poison?

'Vodka lime and soda, which would have been around in the seventies, though I'd have been out of my head on it if anybody had given me any!

Running a backstreet boozer in any decade – especially one frequented by rowdy testosterone-fuelled lawmen letting off steam after various close calls or celebrating collars – requires a combination of good humour, diplomacy and a willingness to adopt strong-arm tactics when needed. Tony himself has never been in any trouble, never left an establishment except under his own steam…?

'I've never been thrown out of a pub, no. I'm always far too well behaved, me, even though I'm a Northern lad!'

As the purveyor of favourite tipples from foaming ales to single malts did Tony ever manage to sneak any … *exciting* beverages on to the set, or was it cold tea all the way?

'I never smuggled the real thing, no – although I have to say if I was going to sneak anything into the world of the Railway Arms it would have been a busty barmaid rather than a drink!'

Harder to fit in the pocket, though.

'But more fun trying!'

Like good barmen everywhere, Nelson dispenses words of wisdom as readily as a pint of bitter or a Cinzano and lemonade. If Tony were drinking in the Railway Arms, what advice would he give himself?

'Treat everyone the way you want to be treated – you'll get back what you'll give out. Yeah, definitely.'

Nelson has an uncanny ability to give the simplest of statements a layer of meaning beyond the words themselves, and his gentle, laconic wisdom provides an oasis of calm in Sam's fractured existence.

His first full conversation with Sam, in Episode One, sets out his philosophical stall:

**SAM:** Large whisky please.
**NELSON:** Drink ain't gonna fix things.
  *NELSON realises what he's said.*
**NELSON:** What am I saying'? I run a pub! Of course it will fix things!
  *He laughs. His laugh is so infectious SAM has to grin. NELSON'S grin fades away.*
**SAM:** I'm lost Nelson. Really lost.
  *NELSON looks to the other end of the bar and then leans in close to SAM, all very serious. And when he speaks, the broad Rasta lilt is gone. NELSON has a soft, firm Lancashire brogue.*
**NELSON:** You're not lost pal. You're where you are. And you have to make the best of it. It's all you can do.
  *SAM doesn't know what to say - NELSON's accent change has thrown him. He looks behind him confused. Is this the same man?*

Mind you, sometimes even Nelson is at a loss. He is mystified when Sam produces a television [confiscated from a bunch of hippies who are fencing electrical goods] and places it on the bar in Episode Four:

**NELSON:** What is that, *mon brave*?
**GENE:** It's a television.
  *NELSON looks baffled.*
**NELSON:** In a pub?
  *GENE gestures towards SAM.*
**GENE:** Yeah, ask the boy wonder here.
**SAM:** It's nothing to do with me.
**GENE:** Oi, tell him what you told me.
**SAM:** (Sheepish) Well, I could make some brackets and we could put it on the wall...and watch the sport.
**NELSON:** (baffled) In a pub??

Those were the days, when the hubbub of pub conversation was broken only by the *thunk* of dart on dartboard, the flash, beep and clatter of the one-armed bandit or the sound of breaking glass as an evening's quiet relaxation descended into fisticuffs. Still, the pub is at the heart of every community and *Life On Mars* is no exception. Not an episode passes without CID repairing to the Railway Arms at some point to scrub away the taste of a crooked Manchester with warm beer and peanuts. Just as they contemplate at the end of Episode Eight, after Sam has gone AWOL on duty, learned the bitter truth about his father, and finally failed to get home. Oh, and Sam and Gene have each pulled a gun on the other.

**RAY:** So. What d'you want to do now, Guv?
  *GENE takes a deep breath and turns to RAY.*
**GENE:** Pub.
  *RAY turns to GENE.*
**RAY:** Pub.
  *CHRIS smiles at SAM.*
**CHRIS:** Pub.
  *SAM hesitates, then smiles and adds:*
**SAM:** Pub.

# SAM'S JOURNEY
## Looking for Clues

*'My name is Sam Tyler.*
*I had an accident, and I woke up in 1973.*
*Am I mad, in a coma, or back in time?*
*Whatever's happened, it's like I've landed on a different planet.*
*Now maybe if I can work out the reason, I can get home...'*

Sam's voiceover, as heard over the title sequence, Episodes 2-8

### EPISODE ONE

Reeling from the shock of finding himself in 1973, doubting his sanity, and struggling to cope without computers, mobile phones, DNA testing, sophisticated forensics or any of the normal paraphernalia of his job, Sam is still a detective to his core, and when a girl is found murdered in Satchmore Road – the very place from which his present-day colleague and girlfriend, Maya, was snatched when she got too close to a serial killer – his policeman's instincts immediately kick in.

Although he gets off on the wrong foot with Gene, and his new colleagues are mystified by his methods, Sam succeeds in solving the case: score one to him. He also makes the connection between the 1973 murder and the present day – but, trapped in 1973, there is no way he can use his new-found knowledge to help Maya. Or is there?

Sam is in possession of a crucial medical document which, if he destroys it, could prevent the early release of the killer, Edward Kramer. If Kramer is still banged up in prison in the future, then Maya will be safe.

Torn between duty and conscience, Sam destroys the document, thereby taking a step into Gene's world. 'Welcome to the team,' says Gene. 'Thanks, guv,' Sam replies.

■ FLASHBACK. While Sam loses consciousness in the road after he is hit by the car he sees, briefly, small black patent leather buckled shoes and a flash of red through the leaves of a sunlit wood, and hears a child's voice saying, 'Where are you?'

■ FUTURE BLEED. The maths lecturer on the television in Sam's room begins to talk about Sam in medical terms, apparently channelling a doctor. 'I have to stress that Sam is in low responsiveness,' he begins, 'but is not in a persistent vegetative state...' causing Sam to pound on the television screen, shouting, 'Look at me! Does this look like low responsiveness to you?' But the doctor, unable to hear him, fades out, to Sam's distress, leaving the static Test Card on the screen.

■ SAM/ANNIE. As a woman Annie is naturally more sympathetic to Sam than the men on the CID team, and he feels instinctively able to confide in her from the start. 'I'm not mad,'

he insists: 'I had an accident, and I woke up 33 years in the past...' As a psychology graduate Annie copes with this information with more equanimity than most. She firmly believes that Sam is deluded, but sets about gently to persuade him that concussion from his RTA is the cause. Her efforts to convince him, however, backfire when her fellow psychology student – and ex-boyfriend – Neil, attempts to jolt Sam out of it by telling him that he

*is* unconscious, he *is* in a hospital bed and that, if he listens to instructions, he can make himself wake up. Sam interprets the 'definitive step' he needs to take as meaning he should throw himself off the roof of CID, since, if he destroys the 1973 persona he has created, which is only fictional in any case, his conscious self will return to the present day.

■ THE REAL NEIL?  Neil appears as if from nowhere when Sam is alone in the canteen. Sam rubs his hands over his tired eyes, and when he looks up again Neil is there. He could have sat quietly down while Sam – and we – couldn't see him. On the other hand, it's a long way from the canteen door to Sam's table. He tells Sam: 'Can you hear me? My name is Neil. I'm a hypnotherapist... At this moment I'm sitting beside you in your bed, in the IC ward of St James's Hospital. Your mobile hasn't stopped ringing,' he reassures Sam, 'and Maya is here.' Afterwards Annie tells Sam that it was all an elaborate ploy, and that Neil got his information from the notes Sam wrote her to show that he knew what was going on in the world in 2006. Sam is not entirely convinced – his notes never mentioned mobile phones, for example – and nor are we.

■ KEY MOMENT. Still, it is Annie who talks Sam down from the roof and persuades him not to jump. 'Maybe you're here for a reason,' she tells him. 'To make a difference.' At the same time, Sam notices when she takes his hand that hers is all grainy with sand. From the fire bucket, she tells him, which she knocked into in her haste as she ran up the stairs to reach him. For the first time Sam begins to doubt that he could have entirely created the world he finds himself in, and that maybe it is real after all. 'Why would I bother to put that level of detail in it?' he wonders.

What would have happened if Sam had jumped? Would he have woken up back in the present, as he intended, or would he be dead? We'll never know. The only thing we do know is that it is Annie's pleading with him that makes him change his mind. 'What should I do, Annie?' he asks her. 'Stay,' she answers. And he does.

## EPISODE TWO

Sam learns the hard way that he is not always right, and that 'doing it by the book' can have unforeseen consequences. Armed robber Kim Trent is high on CID's wanted list, except that once they have finally collared him, they have insufficient evidence to hold him. Sam is horrified to learn that Gene is prepared to plant stolen goods on Trent to keep him off the streets, while Gene is equally disgusted at Sam's sqeamishness, especially when Sam has Trent released.

Trent promptly robs a jewellers shop, in the course of which June, a CID office cleaner, is shot and critically injured.

Sam sees another side of Gene as Gene rounds on him for putting June in danger. This is now personal: she is one of them – and Gene looks after his own. 'I want to be able to look her dad in the eye,' he says, 'and say you cleaned up every drop of her precious blood.' Sam, furious, mortified, blaming Gene as Gene blames him,

tries wildly to scrub her blood from the street with his coat. 'I'm better than any of this,' he protests. 'Says you,' retorts Gene.

Later, by June's hospital bed, they reach an uneasy truce. Sam asks Gene if he wants him out. 'You must be joking,' answers Gene – Sam has to put things right by nailing Trent. 'I only know one way to police,' says Sam. 'So do I,' says Gene. 'She's not giving up,' he goes on, indicating June, 'and nor should you.'

■ In the Railway Arms, Sam asks despairingly, 'Why does it have to be now? Why this particular year?' Why not a year he enjoyed, like 1988. 'Please can I change it?' he shouts, and, for a moment, the lights flicker wildly as if it might be possible, if only he wills hard enough. Annie tells him to leave the pub as Gene is on the warpath. 'I think you should go home,' she tells him. 'Love to,' he says. 'Can't.'

■ SAM/ANNIE. A genuine empathy is starting to develop between Sam and Annie at this point. Annie, however, cannot conceal her hurt that Sam still doesn't seem convinced that she has her own existence outside his head. 'You have to believe in the people around you,' she says. After all, real or not, they are all he has.

■ This episode marks the first appearance of the Test Card Girl outside the television screen. Sam is totally freaked to find her standing large as life in his room, and even more freaked when she tells him: 'I'm sorry you're lonely, Sam. Are you really lonely here? Don't you think it can be lonely out there too? In the white room that's too warm. Life goes on. But does it really go on for the sleeping man? And isn't it better here, where you can be busy?'

■ FUTURE BLEED. Alone in the CID office Sam hears what he believes to be two medics discussing his case. The voices turn out to be part of a radio play. Later when he visits June – herself unconscious – in hospital, all the ward doors slam shut abruptly, trapping him, and he hears two nurses saying that his life support is shutting down because a leaky catheter has shorted the electrics. 'That's what happens when he's left alone too long,' says one. Sam is panicking, yelling for help, certain that he is dying, when he has another memory flash, seeing the patent shoes again and hearing a shrill scream; at which point the doors crash open once more as suddenly as they shut – panic over.

■ GENE MOMENT. Incognito with Sam in a travelling ice cream van, Gene sticks two fingers up at a trio of small girls who ask him for ice cream, causing much wailing and tears. Sam also finds out more about the Hunt philosophy when Gene tells him, 'I've never fitted up anyone who didn't deserve it.' Chris, on the other hand, is just beginning to look on Sam as something of a mentor, as Sam explains his methods.

■ Also in this episode we find out that Ray hates Sam's guts – not only because of their different attitudes to policing, but because Ray was up for Inspector before Sam came on the scene.

■ Sam comes through, protecting Leonard, the deaf witness to the robbery, as much from the ridicule of CID as from Trent, and persuading him to testify so they can put Trent away.

■ In the Railway Arms that evening Gene invites Sam to join his card game for the first time. (Ray, however, gets up and leaves the table when Sam sits down, ostensibly to take a leak). 'Are you sure you're in?' asks Gene. 'Deal me,' Sam replies. He is beginning to accept, and to be accepted.

## EPISODE THREE

The police radio in the Cortina disconcertingly tells Sam that his levels of responsiveness have decreased recently. 'Whatever life-blood is left in your veins, use it. You *must* keep fighting. Keep fighting, Sam.'

And Sam needs every ounce of his tenacity when his instincts run counter to Gene's in the case of a worker's death at Crester's Mill. Gene is positive Ted Bannister is guilty. Sam is just as convinced he's not. Gene bets Sam a tenner and a Watney's Party Seven [a seven-pint can of beer] that he's right. Sam will not reduce a murder inquiry to such a childish level – until Gene says that Sam has no fight; and the bet is on.

The problem is that every lead Sam follows to try and prove Ted's innocence does the reverse. The victim's blood is on his shirt. The bootprint is his. And then he confesses. Nothing but sheer bloody-mindedness leads Sam finally to the truth: that the killer was not a man at all but a faulty textile machine. Ted, in a supreme act of self-sacrifice, was prepared to take the rap to prevent the mill from closure, with the loss of eight hundred jobs. The bitter irony is that Sam, with his future knowledge, is aware that in thirty years time the mill will be gone anyway, along with most of Manchester's heavy industry. Annie says it's a good result: 'Nobody goes down for life.' 'The community goes down for life,' says Sam. 'You don't know that for sure,' says Annie. But he does.

■ A constant theme in this episode is fighting on and not giving in no matter what the odds. Ted Bannister is fighting for his family and their future. Sam is determined to fight for Ted: 'I'm not giving up on this one. I'm gonna fight it. Ted Bannister is not your killer.' Apropos of the mill closure, Sam says: 'The fight's the thing. Without it you go under.' Is this his subconscious talking? And when Chris asks him why he has to deliberately get Gene's goat, his reply is revealing: 'I need to fight, Chris.'

■ DOUBLE MEANINGS. Referring to the giant mill chimney beside which they are standing, Ted Bannister says to Sam, 'Living things need to keep working on the inside. Once the inside stops…' Sam finishes the sentence: '…it's just a shell.'

Later on when Sam is talking to Ted's son Derek, whom fear of the future has driven to desperate measures, he says: 'Look, I know how you're feeling. You feel the walls are closing in on you and you're trapped and you're terrified of what's waiting for you out there.'

■ NELSON. Sam says, 'It's over, Nelson. I'm fighting to stay strong, but I feel like I'm losing.' Nelson answers: 'You're strong. No doubt. But you got to pick your fight, *mon brave*. Who you fighting? Mr Hunt? He really your enemy? …You're fighting because you're scared. Maybe fear is the enemy, hmm? It's not over for you, Sam.'

■ TEST CARD GIRL. The Test Card Girl appears to Sam at night again. 'Do you feel helpless …?' she asks him. 'Unappreciated…? Scared….?' Sam picks up the thread. 'If I stop fighting, then I'm scared I'll die.' 'You poor thing…Give up,' she suggests to him. 'Lie down. Close your eyes. And sleep… No more nastiness. Just sleep. Forever. Sleep.' Sam, desperate for a dreamless and undisturbed sleep, is almost seduced, until the steady beeping of a heart monitor he's been hearing first flatlines and then melds seamlessly into the steady whine of a 1970s television on shutdown. Just in time, he sits bolt upright, insisting, 'No!'

■ FUTURE FLASH. Sam is perturbed to realise that not only is Crester's Mill the site of his flat in the present day, but the body is underneath his kitchen table. He sees a flash of his stainless steel, hi-tech kitchen stained with blood. Later, when foiling a wages snatch at the same site, he sees a confusion of flashes in which Gene, the Test Card Girl, his kitchen and the recurring scene in the woods are all jumbled up.

■ SAM/ANNIE. There's not much opportunity for their relationship to grow in this episode – Sam's too busy. But he does enlist her help on the case, enabling her to use

both her qualifications and her intiative, and causing Gene to comment that she is turning into 'a proper little CID girl'.

■ The role of fathers becomes increasingly significant as the series progresses. In Ted Bannister's house there are two cards on the mantelpiece saying: 'To Daddy' and 'No.1 Dad.'

■ Also in this episode we first learn of the rivalry between CID and the Regional Crime Squad led by DCI Litton. Sam takes another step towards being one of the team when he leads CID in a chant of triumph, telling Litton: 'I think you'd better swallow it down. We had a result. One nil.' Back in the Railway Arms, Sam and Gene open the Watney's Party Seven together.

## EPISODE FOUR

Sam's principles and Gene's pragmatism clash once more when Sam comes up against gangster Stephen Warren, who has the local police firmly in his pocket. Gene explains the system of checks and balances by which they turn a blind eye to Warren's business empire and Warren in turn keeps the streets clear of petty crime. Sam wants none of it – he's seen where a culture of bent coppers leads and the damage it can do. Besides, he says of Warren's unsavoury nature: 'We're not talking about a dodgy telly. We're talking about sexual threats and violence.'

Sure that even Sam is corruptible, Warren sends one of his dancers, Joni, to slip him LSD and seduce him, in order to blackmail him with photographs as a result.

Sam's innate decency and kindness, however, persuade Joni to destroy the photos and try to escape from Warren's clutches for real. Her defiance of Warren costs her her life, and a second time Sam's morality has caused someone else to suffer. Ray says as much to Chris: 'He might as well have slit her throat

himself.' And, to Sam's face: 'If you don't play the game, people get hurt. *You* didn't play the game, and she paid the price.'

On the plus side, Sam's refusal to knuckle under spurs Gene to make his own stand against Warren, and the two of them work together to bring the gangster down. In reply to Sam's asking him how it feels to take backhanders, Gene says it feels like an animal eating away at his insides. 'Fancy doing something about it?' enquires Sam. 'I thought you'd never ask,' says Gene. Afterwards, Gene offers Sam his first words of genuine approbation. 'You did well, Sam. Every officer will be walking a little bit taller tomorrow because of you.'

■ NELSON. Finding a roll of Warren's cash stuffed in his pocket, Sam says to Nelson, 'I'm losing it, Nelson. I'm forgetting who I am in all this madness.' Struggling to hold on to his integrity, he says: 'I just want to go home.' 'Me too, Sam,' sympathises Nelson. 'Close the door on your way out.'

■ VOICES. The television glove puppet Mr Sockley suddenly starts to speak with Sam's mother's voice. 'Sam?' she asks, 'What have they done to my beautiful boy? Can you hear me? Can you hear what I'm saying?' Sam can hear her through the medium of his TV, but she can't hear him respond. 'Sam…don't leave us,' she begs him.

■ PAST, PRESENT AND FUTURE. In this episode Sam revisits his childhood home for the first time since he found himself in 1973. In the street he encounters familiar figures: the Tyler family cat, Ivanhoe, and Alfie, the rag-and-bone collector. He calls on his mother on the pretext of making safety checks in the wake of a spate of burglaries. Clearly drawn to him, although she has no idea why, she makes him tea and talks to him about her son who wants to be a policeman. They are both comfortable and uncomfortable with one another, a situation which disconcerts Sam as much as it puzzles her. Young Sam is upstairs in bed with mumps, but his mother asks adult Sam to come back for tea another time, which he can't resist accepting. Will he meet his four-year-old self? Even if he is a time-traveller, could it really be possible?

■ FLASHBACKS: In the course of his (unwitting) LSD trip Sam sees the woods again, the shoes, a glimpse of red, intercut with the cat Ivanhoe, the Test Card Girl, soldiers, war, images off the television and a naked Joni on top of him. The Test Card Girl says: 'There's nothing to be ashamed of, Sam. You can't be lonely all the time.' Next morning, in the station, before he has fully 'come down' from the effects, he hears his doctors speaking through Ray and Chris: 'His brain functions and heart rate are all up' and: 'It's what we'd expect from a change of medication…'

■ GENE MOMENT. Gene is unsympathetic to Sam's 'honeytrap' plight, summing it up pithily as: 'Pretty girl appealed to your vanity as the only decent sheriff in Dodge City. Slipped you a mickey, tied you up and bounced on your ding-a-ling.'

■ SAM/ANNIE: Annie is shocked and disappointed to find Sam helpless and handcuffed to his bed by Joni. She is cool to him afterwards, but it is clear that she still cares, as she tells him she's decided to be a good friend to him, "Cause with the enemies you're making, you could do with all the friends you can get.' Then she says as she walks away: 'Hey, I got to see you naked. It's not all that bad.'

■ Sam returns to his mother's house in response to her invitation to tea, but it's empty. Ruth and the four-year-old Sam are not there. That night, however, when Sam is asleep, Mr Sockley again speaks from the television with his mother's voice: 'Sleep well, darling. Mum's here. I'll always be here. One day you'll wake up and I'll still be here. I love you…'

## EPISODE FIVE

When a United fan is found face down in a pool of blood, Gene reckons the death is football-related, and that a rival City supporter is to blame. Fuelled by inflammatory press reports, Manchester battens down to prepare for revenge attacks in the hours leading up to the City/United derby. But the circumstances aren't so cut and dried as they first appear, and Sam persuades Gene to go undercover with him and Annie in the United supporters' pub, the Trafford Arms, in pursuit of his hunch that this particular murder is both more and less than it seems.

As it turns out, Gene and Sam are both right – the case *is* football-related, but not in the way that Gene assumed; and the identity of the killer surprises everyone, not least Sam.

But Sam succeeds in bringing potentially warring sides together: the spectre of violence has been defused and supporters of both teams can – for now, at least – co-exist in peace.

■ ONCE A RED. There is an underlying theme to do with belonging in this episode. Pete Bond makes an impassioned defence of what it means to follow a football team: 'Once a Red, always a Red … it makes you feel like you really belong to something.' When Sam fails to connect with the other supporters in the pub, complaining, 'They're not very friendly,' Gene tells him: 'That's because you're not their kind of people.' Sam, put out, asks who *is* their kind of people. 'Me,' says Gene.

■ FATHERS AND SONS. Sam befriends the teenage son of the murder victim, remembering how he once went to matches with his own father, before his dad walked out on him and his mum when he was four. He tells Ryan: 'If you stop doing all the things you used to do with your dad, you lose him all over again. And that thing you're feeling now – it will never go away.'

■ In fact, Sam realises, the last match he ever went to with his dad as a kid was this very weekend in 1973.

■ TEST CARD GIRL. The night after Sam makes a promise to Ryan that he will find the killer, Test Card Girl comes to life once more – this time she's sitting on top of Sam's TV. 'Why did you promise him, Sam?' she says, and: 'Daddies always let you down, don't they?' at which point he sees the shoes and the sunlit woods again, the flash of red and the sudden scream…

■ GENE MOMENT. To set up their cover story, Gene orders Ray to arrest the landlord of the Trafford Arms. 'What for?' asks Ray, understandably. 'Think of something on the way,' says Gene. Later, installed in the pub, Gene asks Sam: 'So, what have you found out, apart from how much lemonade to put in a tart's Dubonnet?'

■ RAY MOMENT. Standing by the murder

victim's dead body, Ray asks, 'Shall I go and let his old lady know she can join the singles club?'

■ DOUBLE MEANING. While the rest of the United fans get rowdy in the Trafford Arms, mild-mannered Pete Bond gets friendly with Sam, telling him at one point: 'You look like a man wishing you were somewhere else.'

■ LEARNING CURVE. Sam is forced to acknowledge that, however unorthodox his methods, Gene knows what he's doing. Thinking that Gene is paralytic drunk in the Trafford Arms, Sam hauls him out of the bar and starts to lay into him verbally, only to find it was all an act which Gene put on to get in with the fans. 'How do you think I became a DCI…?' snaps the instantly sober – and very angry – Gene. 'What, you think they give away badges in them lucky bags? Seeing that Sam is suitably chastened, Gene goes on: '… let's finish what we started. And if I want a bollocking for drinking too much, I'll phone the wife. Are we done?' Later on, when Gene squares up to hard man Malcolm Cox, Pete Bond comments to Sam: 'Your mate's got some balls.' 'If they were any bigger,' says Sam with grudging respect, 'he'd need a wheelbarrow.'

■ POLICING ACCORDING TO GENE. Under-cover in the Trafford Arms, Gene decks a customer and knocks him unconscious, ostensibly for not paying his tab. Dragging him into the kitchen, Gene explains to Sam, 'I arrested him three months ago for assault.' 'Did you have to hit him?' asks Sam. 'Well,' says Gene, 'I thought it were a good idea, just before he said "Hello Detective Chief Inspector, fancy seeing you here."'

■ SAM/ANNIE. The two of them are back on a footing of friendly flirtatious banter, although early on, Sam says, 'Long time no see' and Annie says (smilingly) 'That's 'cause I've been avoiding you.' They clearly enjoy working together as equals behind the bar in the Trafford Arms, away from the constraints of CID.

■ At the end, watching United and City supporters go to the match together, Sam's eye is caught by a small boy, about four years old, in a red-and-white hat and scarf; and a voice says: 'You excited about the match, Sam?'

## EPISODE SIX

Sam picks up a ringing phone – apparently disconnected – in the CID office, only to hear his mother's voice on the other end. 'I've let you down,' she says. 'I know you can't hear me, but it doesn't make this any easier.' 'They showed me a scan of your brain,' she tells him. 'They look for these patches of colour, and there's nothing, Sam.' He is saying down the phone, 'For God's sake, Mum, get better doctors…' but of course she can't hear him. 'You're breathing, but it's an illusion of life. I know you've already gone somewhere else now.'

'Oh god,' pleads Sam. 'Don't say it.' But she goes on: 'I've given my consent to turn it off…this afternoon. Two o'clock. Sleep tight, darling…'

Sam is terrified, desperate – and it's not made any easier when Phyllis tells him a man is holding hostages at gunpoint – and threatening that at two o'clock, someone will have to die.

Sam is determined that no-one must die – not the hostages, not the hostage-taker, and certainly not him – but it takes all his ingenuity to prevent his trigger-happy colleagues from storming the building; negotiate with the hostage-taker, and make sure everyone gets out alive – especially after he, Gene and Annie all become prisoners of the jittery, angry gunman.

■ GENE MOMENT: Sam, worried that there will be a bloodbath unless the correct techniques are used to defuse the crisis, insists: 'I'm the negotiator.' 'I'll make you a hat,' replies Gene.

■ VOICES: As the clock ticks down to 2 p.m. Sam hears intermittent hospital voices discussing his imminent switch-off: 'You can withdraw the feeding tube now. We'll disconnect at two.' And again: 'We'll remove his catheter. Call the nurse.'

■ DOUBLE MEANINGS. These occur mostly through Reg, the troubled gunman, in this episode. He says, 'Some people are the living dead, and don't even know it. I woke up one morning, and I realised it.' Later Sam says to him, 'You feel isolated.' 'Like the Connecticut Yankee at the Court of King Arthur,' agrees Reg, referencing the Mark Twain novel. 'A man out of time.' And at one minute to two, Reg tells Sam: 'You're deluded, Sam. You're breathing, your heart's beating, but it's an illusion of life. You're dead already. Time to put you out of your misery.' Also *Manchester Gazette* reporter and fellow-hostage Jackie Queen says to Sam at one point: 'You're in the wrong institution, Inspector.' 'You don't know the half of it!' Sam replies.

■ NO MORE HEROES? There's an underlying theme throughout this episode of what exactly constitutes a hero: a theme which touches at one point or another on the actions of Annie, Gene and Reg as well as Sam.

■ JACKIE QUEEN. 'Ask Jackie Queen if she thinks we're heroic,' says Gene. It is obvious there is some bad blood between them. Sam learns that Gene once mistakenly shot what he thought was an armed robber, who turned out to be an unarmed kid – a mistake that has been on his conscience ever since. Jackie wrote up the unvarnished truth. 'All the *Gazette* ever asked for was greater police accountability,' she argues. 'You turned it into a hatchet job,' says Gene, 'and I had to live that down.'

■ CHEATING DEATH? Handcuffed to the radiator and waiting to be shot, Annie suggests they each remember the best moments of their lives. Gene says, 'I don't think about my past.' Sam – after a false start in which the only highlights he can think of are to do with work – remembers his fourth birthday, waiting anxiously for his dad to come home after a time away, thinking that he was going to be disappointed – and then, the ecstatic relief of knowing that his dad was there after all. As the clock ticks down, Sam sees the woods and the shoes and hears the voice again: 'Where are you?' But at 2 o'clock precisely, the full recall of that wonderful fourth birthday – hearing his dad's voice, not even needing to turn around to see him – makes Sam laugh, and at that moment, CID and RCS burst in and the siege is over – although not before Gene takes a bullet to the chest, and is saved by the hip-flask

in his breast pocket.

■ SAM/ANNIE. They are too preoccupied with events to let their feelings show throughout most of this episode, except in the last few minutes of the siege, when, convinced they really are going to die, emotion breaks through as they offer each other what small comfort they can. Afterwards Sam asks Annie why they didn't switch him off, why he cheated death, and she says, 'Sam – do me a favour. Enjoy the moment.'

■ Later, in the Railway Arms, the red trimphone on the bar rings, and only Sam seems aware of it. Picking it up, he hears his mother again, speaking to the hospital staff: 'I don't care what your machine says. I'm leaving him on. You say you can't detect anything, but I know what I saw! At two o'clock on the dot, I saw Sam smile.' The line falters and the operator's voice breaks in: 'Operator; can I connect you?' 'I was just connected,' Sam says with a happy grin.

## EPISODE SEVEN

A death in custody threatens to shatter the fragile equilibrium Sam has reached both in the station and in 1973. Gene seems determined to hush it up but Sam can't let it lie. As he probes deeper to find out who was to blame, the whole station closes ranks, and Sam is more of an outsider now than he was when he first arrived. Even Annie is defensive and seems to resent his questioning.

'Is this what you do?' asks Gene bitterly. 'Bust through stations, ripping them apart, destroying the camaraderie?' Sam's justification is simple: 'If we can't police ourselves, how is the public supposed to trust us?'

Eventually his persistence reveals what his colleagues are hiding: Ray force-fed the suspect cocaine to get him to talk, not knowing he had a weak heart – and Chris has the proof on tape. But Sam is gobsmacked to discover that Gene intended all along that he should find out the truth of what happened. Gene could hardly investigate his own team; and Sam was the one he trusted to do the job. Besides, says Gene, 'isn't that how you've always fancied yourself? The moral compass in a dodgy department?'

Sam wants Ray charged. Gene refuses. 'Ray Carling catches more villains than the rest of this department put together. I boot him out, dozens of villains go uncollared.' Sam is outraged, but Gene has another, more compelling reason. 'I'm to blame for this,' he confesses. 'These lads, they think they're made in my image, but they've never learned where to draw the line, and it scares the shit out of me.' Instead, he strips Ray of his rank in a public humiliation, and docks half his pay for the next twelve months. As far as Gene is concerned, the matter is over.

But not for Sam. Still driven by his moral imperatives, he takes the evidence to their Superintendent, who destroys it – he too considers that Gene has done whatever needs to be done. Internal discipline is sufficient: there is no need to let it out into the public domain. Gene is philosophical. 'You can't change this

world, Sam,' he says. 'Only learn how to survive in it. 'I don't give up that easily,' Sam warns. 'Good,' says Gene.

■ FUTURE FLASH: When Gene and Sam go out to eat 'to discuss procedure' Sam is momentarily blinded by a flashing light and hears a voice ask: 'Is he responding?' For a second he sees the restaurant as it is in the present day, with Britney Spears booming out of it and the neon-lit twenty-first century street reflected in its window. Inside, he hears Pulp's 'Disco 2000' coming from the radio and then a voice saying, 'The way Sam responds to these sensory tests will be crucial.'

■ TESTS. The thread of Sam being tested runs throughout the episode. In the gents at CID he suddenly tastes Tabasco on his tongue, gagging into the sink as a voice says: 'There's no discernable reaction.' He sees the black shoes and a woman in red running, and the voice says, 'We need some response to these tests. He has to help us.' Sam flips totally at this point and yells at the top of his voice, 'Get me out of here'

– a moment of weakness overheard by Ray.

■ KEY MOMENT. Later on in the Railway Arms Sam has an epiphany: he has to destroy Gene's world to get back to his. 'That's how they want me to respond,' he convinces himself. 'Maybe the tests are working. Maybe I'm close to getting home.' No tie he's forged in 1973 can hold him – not even Annie. If bringing them down is the key, he won't hesitate to do it. This is the real reason behind his decision to give the tape to Rathbone – and why he is so desolate when Rathbone destroys the tape. There is no going home for him this time – he now has no means to demolish this world, so what he was sure would be his route home is closed. He is stuck here, with all his colleagues – Annie included – aware that he was prepared to ruin their careers.

■ NELSON. Sam asks, 'What am I doing, Nelson? Why am I still fighting?' 'Nobody else is bothered about the truth,' he says, despairingly. 'Why should I be?' Nelson answers: 'You've always got to follow the truth, even if it brings the whole damn thing crashing around you,' inadvertently triggering Sam's revelation.

■ GENE MOMENT. Arguing in the gents, Gene has Sam pinned face down against the basin with his arm twisted behind his back when Superintendent Rathbone walks in on them and, without missing a beat, comments: 'Staff training *à la* Gene Hunt?' Rathbone reckons that Gene is a double-edged sword. 'Plenty would like to see your head on a pole, Gene,' he warns him. 'I've sheltered you one too many times.' 'I think I know where I stand,' says Gene. 'Right on the edge,' Rathbone replies, 'wobbling.'

■ DOUBLE MEANINGS. Referring to Sam's threat to 'go back to Hyde' Gene informs him: 'You could have gone back any time you fancied. The truth is you like it here – you just can't bear to admit it.' Later on, before Sam takes the tape to Rathbone, Gene says: 'The power's in your hands. You've got the tape. You can still destroy us, if that's what you want.' And when Rathbone crushes the tape in his hands, he says to Sam, coldly: 'What were you expecting, Tyler? The whole world to come crashing down?'

■ Ironically, it is Chris doing what Sam taught him – taping interviews – that finally leads Sam to Ray, and gives him the concrete proof with which to tear Gene's team apart.

■ The Open University lecturer appears on the TV again in this episode. 'And the answer to the problem is clearer than we might think. This could be a turning point,' he asserts, just as Sam is deciding whether to use the tape or not. Sam is shouting, 'Help me. Tell me what to do…' but there's no answer, as the TV fizzes into static.

■ SAM/ANNIE: Breaking into Annie's locker to find the tape, Sam can't resist burying his face in her spare uniform, drinking in her scent. But for her part Annie doesn't appreciate Sam's

investigation. 'Friendship and trust goes both ways, Sam, you know. Or it's supposed to.' Later, when she learns what he plans to do, she tells him. 'We're people. We have lives, we're not some game created just for your benefit. You think you give that tape to the Super and we just melt away?' Her message is unequivocal: 'We have to live with what we did. We don't need you to punish us. You've got my career, my life, in your hands.'

Afterwards he tells her: 'I had to do it.' She says, sadly: 'So I do mean that little to you.' 'Why am I still here?' he asks her. 'Nothing I do makes any difference.' 'Is that what you really think?' she asks, and walks away. 'Don't abandon me, please,' he says to her. 'How would I do that?' she responds 'We're stuck here together. Back to work is it?' she asks him. 'Do I have a choice?' he answers. 'Park? Pictures?' she tells him. 'There's always a choice.'

## EPISODE EIGHT

All Sam's instincts for policing desert him when CID, in pursuit of the Mortons, mysterious criminal racketeers, follow a lead which takes them to a hotel room – and the man inside it is Vic Tyler, his father.

Sure that his father is innocent, Sam believes his task is to prove it; thereby enabling Vic to stay with him and his mother instead of leaving them, as he did when Sam was four years old. Obsessed with saving him from whatever he may have got mixed up in, Sam is blind to all the clues which point to his father's guilt, to the extent that, when Gene tries to persuade him to look at the evidence, Sam accuses Gene of wanting to set his father up.

Not until Annie's life is at stake when she tries to prevent Vic from running does Sam accept that his father might be other than he remembers ('When I was little,' he says at one point, 'my dad worked away a fair bit. I used to look for the sight of his jacket on the banister. It was the most exciting thing in the world.') And not until Vic has tried to shoot him in cold blood does he fully accept that his dad is not just a criminal, but a man who is casually capable of murder.

Perhaps his task is not to save Vic but to arrest and expose him for what he is. Vic, however has one last card up his sleeve. As Sam begins to read him his rights, he asks him: 'Are you going to tell Ruth and little Sammie what I am? Or do you want them to read about it in the papers? Find out that daddy's a crook from the kids in the playground? You'll ruin their lives...' Torn every which way, Sam lets Vic go. He can't save him – but nor can he turn him in. Has he just blown the only chance he had of getting home? It certainly feels like that to Sam, as nothing has changed, his father is gone, and he is still in 1973.

■ TEST CARD GIRL. The episode opens with her asking Sam: 'You've done everything you can think of, and you're still no closer to home. Why are you still here, Sam?' Sam is insistent: 'I'm here for a reason.'

■ KEY MOMENT. Full of hope from seeing Vic in the hotel room, Sam says to Annie: 'You know I've been searching for an answer, why I'm here and ... how I get back. Maybe the answer's found me.' Working it out, he speculates: '...he was scared of the Mortons, and that's why he left us.' His father's absence left a void in Sam's childhood, and Sam comes to a decision: 'Maybe that's why I'm here – to stop him from leaving.

History's repeating itself, but I can change it.' Annie asks him what he intends to do. Sam is quite clear: 'Save him – and that'll save me.'

■ FLASHBACKS. In the hotel room, Sam has a flashback to his mum telling him: 'Daddy's gone away, Sammy. He didn't want to, but he had to...' Several times in this episode he also has the vision of the woods and the shoes and the glimpse of the red dress – and each time it happens, he sees a little more. First a dark sleeve, and then a fleeting impression of a man's face, contorted in anger – and the man is Vic. Finally he sees the woman in red being savagely kicked and beaten – and suddenly, horribly, Sam understands. The small patent shoes and the voice, 'Where are you?' are his, aged four, as he follows his father into the woods and sees him attack the woman in the red dress – Annie – a memory he has blanked out ever since.

■ DOUBLE MEANING: While being questioned, Vic mentions that he has a young son called Sam. Sam asks what he's like. 'Oh,' says Vic, 'he's always busy, up here (indicating his head). You know what little nippers are like, all that make believe.'

■ Sam dials a phone number found in a club which was linked to the porn racket run, he assumes, by the Mortons. A small child's voice answers, saying: 'Hello. Sam Tyler speaking. Can I help you?' Utterly rattled, Sam slams the receiver down. Not only has he had the totally unexpected shock of hearing his four-year-old self on the end of the line, but the number is incontrovertible proof – or it should be – that Vic is in much deeper than he's let on.

■ At one point, Vic asks Sam, 'Who *are* you?' Sam says, 'A second chance.' It's almost as if Vic has realised that Sam is not what he seems – he can see that Sam knows a lot of things about him and Ruth and their lives – but it doesn't stop him from aiming a gun at Sam when the chips are down.

■ VOICES. In the station, Sam apparently hears a racing commentator break off mid-race and (still in rapid-fire commentary style) say: 'And we've seen a marked improvement in Sam's condition. There's no doubt about that as we watch his vital signs begin to stabilise. We've recorded a significant increase in brain activity recently, a crucial step towards regaining consciousness…' Later on, thinking he has convinced Vic to stay with his family and not to run, he hears what sound like hospital noises and says out loud: 'That's it. I've done it. I've done it. He's staying. That's it, wakey-wakey!' A voice says: 'Doctor – he moved,' and Sam responds: 'Too right he moved! He's sorted it all out in his head and now he's coming home!' 'Get the team in here' says the voice. 'Yeah, get 'em in, get 'em all in,' shouts Sam. 'Gather round for the big waking up! Come on, gather round, game on…' The machine noises accelerate – but nothing happens. In the sudden silence, Sam, desolate, says: 'I thought I'd done it. I thought he was going to stay. It's going to happen all over again.' Later, as he confronts his dad and is on the cusp of either letting him go or arresting

him, the voices tell him: 'Come on, Sam … He's waking up … Come on.'

■ SAM/ANNIE. As the woman in the red dress who has haunted his flashbacks ever since he first arrived in 1973, Annie is the catalyst who leads Sam to the truth about his father – a truth he has suppressed for thirty-three years. Sam may still be trapped in the past, but Annie's presence is comfort and compensation. At the very end, she says to him: 'Sam…nothing can make you wake up, because you're already awake.' 'I'm never going to believe that,' he warns her. 'But you should know,' he says, reaching out to touch her cheek, 'I don't hate everything about this place.'

# LOST AND FOUND:
# THE WRITING ON THE WALL

Not so long ago Thompson had had the experience of waking up on a public bench and being baffled at the disorientation; at the unfamiliar sense of abandon, of being adrift.

It was getting to be a habit.

This time he had the added 'wrongness' of having to peel his cheek from a carpet. Two items that really shouldn't ever be stuck to one another. Like tar and kittens.

'Which one of you bastards gave me that last gin?' is what his brain ordered his vocal cords to say; though, in reality, all that came out was a sound not dissimilar to the dying breath of an aged vole. It was a question that troubled nobody, least of all DCI Gene Hunt, who was snoring on his back underneath the next table.

Deep in Chris Skelton's sleeping brain Thompson's attempt at speech tickled a synapse, 'Alright!' he shouted, mistaking the half-registered sound for his mother's voice calling him. 'I'm up! I'm up!' Gravity finally woke him – in the sense that he was *asleep* when the table he was lying on toppled over from his rocking but *awake* by the time it had hit the ground.

It was the start of the chain reaction: Chris's foot connected with DC Ray Carling's chin, who in turn jolted up in surprise and slammed his hand into Sam Tyler's stomach, causing Tyler to bellow a choking cough into Adams's ear.

Within seconds the bar of The Railway Arms had turned from a peaceful haven of snoring and mumbling – albeit one with the thick air of a teenager's mattress, all musk and hormones – to a sorry dive of moaning and the rubbing of heads.

The table that Gene had been sleeping under flew ceiling-wards as he got to his feet rather too suddenly, fists up and ready for a fight. Taking in the sea of broken police officers and assessing the threat level at minimum, he lowered his hands and straightened his camel coat.

'Right. Gene needs three things!' he announced. 'Firstly...' he pulled his hipflask out of his pocket. 'Hair of the dog to get the brain turning over.' He took a large shot and gasped his appreciation at the punch of single malt on a morning stomach. 'Secondly, a farm's worth of fried pig on sliced white with lashings of HP, maybe an egg or three to give it consistency.' He belched and clutched his gut. 'But most of all, Gene needs the trap, as he has something brewing that'll be scaring cod between here and Greenland for the next fortnight. Rendezvous at the Cortina in five.' His stomach rumbled audibly. 'Make that ten.' He marched over the still-waking bodies, grabbing a copy of last night's paper off one of the tables as he passed. 'Nelson! I'm commandeering the lav on important police business. Clear the area.'

Stumbling into the chill of a Manchester morning, Adams and Thompson brushed the crust of last night's drunken unconsciousness from their eyes and gazed out at the smoke filled skies of their yesterday.

'Just another day inside my broken head,' Adams sighed.

'Or mine,' Thompson smiled.

They stepped aside as Sam Tyler pushed past them and walked towards the Cortina to radio through the breakfast order to control.

'Or his,' they both said, looking at one another.

Moving away from the gathering officers, Adams took a cigarette out of his pocket, lit then choked on it for a few seconds – that morning hit.

'Whoever's head it is, it's getting comfier and comfier,' he said between puffs. 'If we ever expect to get out of here, we're not exactly going the right way about it.'

'How do you mean?'

Adams sat on the kerb to finish his cigarette. 'We're not fighting. We're getting deeper and deeper, more and more a part of this world.'

Thompson nodded, 'I sort of hoped that we'd fade out once we'd finished, y'know? Once we'd talked to everyone we needed to.'

'Yeah,' Adams looked up at the brick hulk of the building in front of him. Some form of factory he assumed, soot-stained and graffitied. 'The signs of that are not good, though.' He pointed up at the wall in front of them.

Thompson followed his gaze. It took him a second to realise what his colleague was pointing out, then it clicked... 'Oh.'

'Yeah. Guess we're here for a while yet, eh?'

'You ponces need a lift?' Hunt shouted from the door of the pub, heading towards his car.

Adams and Thompson looked at one another and shared a sigh. Thompson turned to shout.

'Yeah, thanks!'

They got to their feet and walked over towards the Cortina, heads hanging low, beneath the painted words that sprawled across the building next to them. There really was very little ambivalence in their meaning, very little room for multiple interpretation…

# NORTH WEST DISTRICT POLICE

## CASE FILE

SERIES ONE
EPISODE ONE

Co-Created By
Matthew Graham
Tony Jordan
Ashley Pharoah

WRITTEN BY MATTHEW GRAHAM
PRODUCED BY CLAIRE PARKER
DIRECTED BY BHARAT NALLURI

| | |
|---|---|
| DCI GENE HUNT | PHILIP GLENISTER |
| DI SAM TYLER | JOHN SIMM |
| DS RAY CARLING | DEAN ANDREWS |
| DC CHRIS SKELTON | MARSHALL LANCASTER |
| WPC ANNIE CARTWRIGHT | LIZ WHITE |

DCI Sam Tyler's world is well defined. It is a world of internet, mobile phones, social workers and regulations. It's about crossing 't's, dotting 'I's and making sure the paperwork's been rubberstamped in triplicate. He lives by it, thrives on it. But none of it means a thing when his colleague and girlfriend, Maya, is kidnapped by a suspected serial killer. Breaking down by the side of the road, his world takes one last blow as he accidentally steps into the path of an oncoming car.

He should be dead.

Instead he awakes to find himself in 1973 and a DI on his first day in a new precinct. His new DCI, Gene Hunt, is everything he hates - a violent, misogynistic creature of instinct.

With ghostly sounds of the future ringing in his head he finds himself struggling to adapt in this alien world. But somehow he's got to find his feet because the case he and Hunt are working on just may be the key to everything - including the safety of Maya.

Will he be able to hold on to his sanity long enough to solve it?

Original Broadcast Stats

Run Time:     59' 00"
Transmission: Monday 9th January 2006,
              9pm BBC ONE

Viewing Figures for original broadcast:
Overnight:              7 million
Adjusted Ratings:       75 million
Audience Share:         28.3%

Adjusted figures include time-shift recordings.

INT. POLICE STATION - CID - DAY 1/2 15:25

Bustle, noise, radios playing. Wads of cast-gum thrown from hand to hand. Huge cast-iron typewriters thumping away. SAM sits amongst it all looking grey and lost.

SAM fumbles for the big grey telephone. He takes a moment to remember it then starts dialling a number.

                    OPERATOR
      Operator.
                    SAM
      What? I'm trying to reach a mobile
      number. 07700 900 813 ..
                    OPERATOR
      Is that an international number?
                    SAM
      I want to connect with a Virgin
      number. A Virgin ...
                    OPERATOR
      Don't you start that sexy business
      with me young man. I can trace this
      call ...

SAM slaps the phone down.

5 1 8 1

Sam Tyler
(AKA John Simm)

**Previous Form:**
Sex Traffic
State of Play
24 Hour Party People
Crime and Punishment
Clocking Off
Human Traffic
The Lakes
Cracker

Gene Hunt
(AKA Philip Glenister)

**Previous Form:**
Vincent
Island at War
Calendar Girls
State of Play
Hornblower
Clocking Off

| | |
|---|---|
| Stunt Co-ordinators | Peter Brayham |
| | Stuart Clarke |
| Stunt Performers | Michael Byrch |
| | Crispin Leyfield |
| | Derek Lea |
| 1st Assistant Director | Simon Turner |
| 2nd Assistant Director | Guy Barker |
| 3rd Assistant Director | Ellena Harris |
| Floor Runner | Thomas Alibone |
| Production Co-ordinator | Michael Noble |
| Assistant Co-ordinator | Tricia Carr |
| Production Office Runner | Lucy Patrick Ward |
| Continuity | Angie Pontefract |
| Production Accountant | Diane Pontefract |
| Assistant Accountant | Matthew Pope |
| Location Manager | Brett Wilson |
| Unit Manager | Joseph Cairns |
| Camera Operator | Nick Beek-Sanders |
| Focus Puller | Carl Hudson |
| Clapper Loader | Kim Tunstall |
| Grip | Ron Fleet |
| Sound Maintenance | Paul Watson |
| Gaffer | Brian Jones |
| Best Boy | Terry Eden |
| Electrician | Danny Griffiths |
| Genny Operator | Tony O'Brien |
| Art Director | Matthew Gant |
| Standby Art Director | Katy Tuxford |
| Art Dept Assistant | Nick Ainsworth |
| Production Buyer | Ian Tully |
| Props Master | Joe Malone |
| Dressing Props | John Fegan |
| | Peter O'Rourke |
| Standby Props | Neil O'Rourke |
| | Pete Moran |
| Standby Carpenter | Gary McCabe |
| Construction Manager | Hugo Slight |
| Police Advisor | Steve Crimmins |
| Costume Supervisor | Monica Aslanian |
| Costume Assistants | Becky Davies |
| | Joanne Evans |

| | |
|---|---|
| MAYA ROY | ARCHIE PANJABI |
| COLIN RAIMES | SAM HAZELDINE |
| YOUNG LAD | HENRY COX |
| RAIMES' LAWYER | CAROLINE HARDING |
| RAIMES' PSYCHIATRIST | PAVEZ QUADIR |
| RAIMES' SOCIAL WORKER | ORLA COTTINGHAM |
| POLICE OFFICER | TOM CHARNOCK |
| NEIL | CHRISTOPHER HARPER |
| TV PRESENTER | RICHARD SINNOTT |
| DORA KEENS | JANE RILEY |
| SID | ANDY ABRAHAMS |
| MRS RAIMES | MAGS GANNON |
| JUNE | RAE KELLY |

| | |
|---|---|
| Make-up Supervisor | Juliet Jackson |
| Make-up Artist | Sarah Rahim |
| Casting Associate | Kirsty Robertson |
| Post Prod Supervisor | Jessica Rundle |
| Assistant Editor | Matt Cannings |
| Online Editor | Justin Eely |
| Colourist | Jet Omoshebi |
| Dialogue Editor | Alex Sawyer |
| Effects Editor | Julian Slater |
| Re-Recording Mixer | Nigel Heath |
| BBC Production Exec | Julie Scott |
| Sound Recordist | Dave Sansom |
| Make-up/Hair Designer | Jessica Taylor |
| Costume Designer | Emma Rosenthal |
| Script Editor | Elwen Rowlands |
| Casting Director | Andy Pryor |
| Production Designer | Brian Sykes |
| Music By | Edmund Butt |
| Editor | Barney Pilling |
| Director of Photography | Adam Suschitzky |
| Line Producer | Marcus Wilson |
| Exec Producers | Jane Featherstone |
| | Matthew Graham |

**NORT**
**DIST**

# CASE FILE

*SERIES ONE*
*EPISODE TWO*

WRITTEN BY MATTHEW GRAHAM
PRODUCED BY CLAIRE PARKER
DIRECTED BY BHARAT NALLURI

| | |
|---|---|
| DCI GENE HUNT | PHILIP GLENISTER |
| DI SAM TYLER | JOHN SIMM |
| DS RAY CARLING | DEAN ANDREWS |
| DC CHRIS SKELTON | MARSHALL LANCASTER |
| WPC ANNIE CARTWRIGHT | LIZ WHITE |
| WPC PHYLLIS DOBBS | NOREEN KERSHAW |

Being on the right side of morality doesn't always get you far.

Kim Trent, an elusive target on the CID's wanted list, is arrested but when Sam finds out that Gene has planted evidence in order to secure a conviction he lets him go, determined not to be a party to the grey-area school of policing he finds all around him.

Gene is furious and stands by the fact that he's never fitted up anyone who didn't deserve it.  Keeping Trent under lock and key guaranteed that the streets would be a little safer without him and, as far as he's concerned, the end justifies the means.

He may be right, as Trent commits an armed robbery, critically wounding June, a young cleaner from the station.

Will Sam be able to track Trent down and get him behind bars without losing the moral high ground?

MUSIC

Live And Let Die – Wings
No One Came – Deep Purple
Drum Song – Willie Lindo & The Charmers Band
Saga Of The Ageing Orphan – Thin Lizzy
Lazy – Deep Purple
One Of These Days – Pink Floyd
Dream Land – The Upsetters

Original Broadcast Stats
Run Time: 57' 30"
Transmission: Monday 16th January 2006,
9pm BBC ONE

Viewing Figures for original broadcast:
Overnight:                    6 million
Adjusted Ratings:         6.3 million
Audience Share:           24%

Adjusted figures include time-shift recordings.

# REGAN STREET

Dear Superintendent Rathbone

It is with some sadness that I am forced to contact you regarding the behaviour of a number of your men last Tuesday.

Whilst I appreciate the good work your chaps do in the name of keeping the streets safe for the likes of myself I am at a loss to understand how a number of the incidents which took place during our Lunch Time Leisure Hour could be seen as constructive.

Staff in our canteen were terrified by what I can only describe as a 'ruckus'. Your officers in their attempt to secure the arrest of their suspect were most insensitive to the feelings of some of the 'Pension Plunge' early birds who were enjoying a cup of our freshly brewed tea at the time. One lady in particular, a long standing visitor to our baths, had to be calmed down for several minutes by my assistant Nigel as she was quite convinced the Germans were invading again. It took several cups of tea and seven (7) lemon puff biscuits to calm her nerves.

Add to this their general behaviour whilst in the pool and their flagrant disobeying of our regulations (the superior officer, DCI Hunt I believe, was seen 'dive-bombing' twice while the officers were awaiting the arrival of the aforementioned suspect, despite our very clear signage telling our visitors not to do so for obvious safety reasons) and I'm afraid we have a state of affairs that has caused a considerable amount of distress, not to mention damage. A full list of breakages is attached.

Whilst I am sure this 'horseplay' does not reflect the general behaviour of the officers under your aegis I nonetheless felt I must contact you both to discuss remuneration and to receive some assurances that this sort of thing won't happen again.

Yours,

*George Newman*

George Newman
(Chief Supervisor)
Regan Street Community Baths

NELSON — TONY MARSHALL
KIM TRENT — ANDREW TIERNAN
DEAF AID — JUNE — RAE KELLY
(AMBULANCE DRIVER — FRANK WALMSLEY
TEST CARD GIRL — RAFAELLA HUTCHINSON
WITNESS — JANE RELPH ←
→ LEONARD — TIMOTHY PLATT
MRS TRENT — SHERRY ORMEROD

TITS IN A JUMPER!

Kim Trent
(AKA Andrew Tiernan)

Previous Form:
Spooks
The Quatermass Experiment
The Rotter's Club
Richard III (2005)
Waking The Dead
The Bunker
Interview With The Vampire
Cracker
Prime Suspect

| | |
|---|---|
| Stunt Co-ordinators | Peter Brayham |
| | Ray L. Nicholas |
| Stunt Performers | Derek Lea |
| | Neil Finnigan |
| 1st Assistant Director | Simon Turner |
| 2nd Assistant Director | Guy Barker |
| 3rd Assistant Director | Ellena Harris |
| Floor Runner | Thomas Alibone |
| Production Co-ordinator | Michael Noble |
| Assistant Co-ordinator | Tricia Carr |
| Production Office Runner | Lucy Patrick Ward |
| Continuity | Angie Pontefract |
| Production Accountant | Diane Pontefract |
| Assistant Accountant | Matthew Pope |
| Location Manager | Brett Wilson |
| Unit Manager | Joseph Cairns |
| Camera Operator | Nick Beek-Sanders |
| Focus Puller | Carl Hudson |
| Clapper Loader | Kim Tunstall |
| Grip | Ron Fleet |
| Sound Maintenance | Paul Watson |
| Gaffer | Brian Jones |
| Best Boy | Terry Eden |
| Electrician | Danny Griffiths |
| Genny Operator | Tony O'Brien |
| Art Director | Matthew Gant |
| Standby Art Director | Katy Tuxford |
| Art Dept Assistant | Nick Ainsworth |
| Production Buyer | Ian Tully |
| Props Master | Joe Malone |
| Dressing Props | John Fegan |
| | Peter O'Rourke |
| Standby Props | Neil O'Rourke |
| | Pete Moran |
| Standby Carpenter | Gary McCabe |
| Construction Manager | Hugo Slight |
| Police Advisor | Steve Crimmins |
| Costume Supervisor | Monica Aslanian |
| Costume Assistants | Becky Davies |
| | Joanne Evans |

| | |
|---|---|
| Make-up Supervisor | Juliet Jackson |
| Make-up Artist | Sarah Rahim |
| Casting Associate | Kirsty Robertson |
| Publicity | Premier PR |
| Post Prod Supervisor | Jessica Rundle |
| Assistant Editor | Matt Cannings |
| Online Editor | Scott Hinchcliffe |
| Colourist | Jet Omoshebi |
| Dialogue Editor | Alex Sawyer |
| Effects Editor | Julian Slater |
| Re-Recording Mixer | Nigel Heath |
| BBC Production Exec | Julie Scott |
| Sound Recordist | Dave Sansom |
| Make-up/Hair Designer | Jessica Taylor |
| Costume Designer | Emma Rosenthal |
| Script Editor | Elwen Rowlands |
| Casting Director | Andy Pryor |
| Production Designer | Brian Sykes |
| Music By | Edmund Butt |
| Editor | Barney Pilling |
| Director of Photography | Adam Suschitzky |
| Line Producer | Marcus Wilson |
| Exec Producers | Jane Featherstone |
| | Matthew Graham |

WEST
T C.I.D

# CASE FILE

SERIES ONE
EPISODE THREE

Co-Created By
Matthew Graham
Tony Jordan
Ashley Pharoah

WRITTEN BY MATTHEW GRAHAM
PRODUCED BY CLAIRE PARKER
DIRECTED BY JOHN MCKAY

| | |
|---|---|
| DCI GENE HUNT | PHILIP GLENISTER |
| DI SAM TYLER | JOHN SIMM |
| DS RAY CARLING | DEAN ANDREWS |
| DC CHRIS SKELTON | MARSHALL LANCASTER |
| WPC ANNIE CARTWRIGHT | LIZ WHITE |
| WPC PHYLLIS DOBBS | NOREEN KERSHAW |

TROUBLE AT
MILL

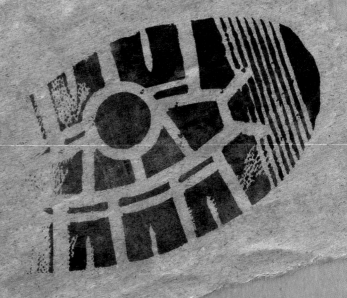

Original Broadcast Stats
  Run Time:    58' 24"
  Transmission: Monday 23rd January 2006,
                9pm BBC ONE

  Viewing Figures for original broadcast:
   Overnight:                     6.2 million
   Adjusted Ratings:              6.5 million
   Audience Share:                25%

     Adjusted figures include time-shift recordings.

There's a rule of thumb in the office of the CID: <u>The first one to speak did it.</u>

When a murder is committed at Crester's Textiles, loom-worker Ted Bannister is the man with the speediest mouth and Gene and his men are only too happy to build a case against him. Sam, ever aware that he's sinking deeper into the world of 1973, isn't convinced and works to prove him innocent.

It doesn't help when all the evidence does seem to point in Bannister's direction.

With only Chris and gut instinct on his side Sam falls back on forensics and solid detective work, positive that Gene has the wrong man.

Then Bannister confesses...

WAGES

C 13/3/73

1385

AMB 1960

MILLING LOOMES (ltd)

*shooting script* extract

INT. POLICE STATION - CORRIDOR - DAY 3/1 12.39

SAM walks like a man with the bit between his teeth. CHRIS trails behind them.

                    SAM
    I want us prepped for mass interviews. Build a
    profile of the mill community. Who hates who.
    Who sleeps with who. Totally open mind at this
    juncture.

                    CHRIS
    What if a gang of 'em all lynched him
    together?

                    SAM
    Could be a gang. Could be trained eagles.
    Could be Ninjas for all we know at this stage.
                    CHRIS
    No way Boss. Not Ninja style.

MUSIC

Ballroom Blitz - Sweet
Gypsy - Uriah Heep
Wishing Well - Free
Head In the Sky - Atomic Rooster

| | |
|---|---|
| NELSON | TONY MARSHALL |
| TINA | REBECCA ATKINSON |
| DEREK BANNISTER | ANDREW KNOTT |
| TED BANNISTER | JOHN HENSHAW |
| ARTHUR COYNES | JOHN AXON |
| DCI LITTON | LEE ROSS |
| DODDS | WARREN DONNELLY |
| BRIAN | NICKY BELL |
| PATHOLOGIST | PAUL LEEMING |
| MRS BANNISTER | DENICE HOPE |
| TEST CARD GIRL | RAFAELLA HUTCHINSON |

GUILTY

GUILTY!

GUILTY

REGIONAL CRIME SQUAD SCUM

Ted Bannister
(AKA John Henshaw)

Previous Form:
Born and Bred
Early Doors
The Second Coming
The Royle Family
Emmerdale
The Grand
Cracker
G.B.H.

| | |
|---|---|
| Stunt Co-ordinators | Ray L. Nicholas |
| Stunt Performers | Gordon Seed |
| | Andy Smart |
| | Paul Howel |
| 1st Assistant Director | Joanna Crow |
| 2nd Assistant Director | Guy Barker |
| 3rd Assistant Director | Ellena Harris |
| Floor Runner | Thomas Alibone |
| Production Co-ordinator | Michael Noble |
| Assistant Co-ordinator | Tricia Carr |
| Production Office Runner | Lucy Patrick Ward |
| Continuity | Angie Pontefract |
| Production Accountant | Diane Pontefract |
| Assistant Accountant | Matthew Pope |
| Location Manager | Brett Wilson |
| Unit Manager | Joseph Cairns |
| Camera Operator | Nick Beek-Sanders |
| Focus Puller | Joe Blackwell |
| Clapper Loader | Kim Tunstall |
| Grip | Ron Fleet |
| Sound Maintenance | Paul Watson |
| Gaffer | Brian Jones |
| Best Boy | Terry Eden |
| Electrician | Danny Griffiths |
| Genny Operator | Tony O'Brien |
| Art Director | Matthew Gant |
| Standby Art Director | Katy Tuxford |
| Art Dept Assistant | Nick Ainsworth |
| Production Buyer | Ian Tully |
| Props Master | Joe Malone |
| Dressing Props | John Fegan |
| | Neil Glynn |
| Standby Props | Neil O'Rourke |
| | Pete Moran |
| Standby Carpenter | Tom Higgins |
| Construction Manager | Hugo Slight |
| Police Advisor | Steve Crimmins |
| Costume Supervisor | Monica Aslanian |

| | |
|---|---|
| Costume Assistants | Becky Davies |
| | Joanne Evans |
| Make-up Supervisor | Juliet Jackson |
| Make-up Artist | Sarah Rahim |
| Casting Associate | Kirsty Robertson |
| Publicity | Premier PR |
| Post Prod Supervisor | Jessica Rundle |
| Assistant Editor | Matt Cannings |
| Online Editor | Scott Hinchcliffe |
| Colourist | Jet Omoshebi |
| Dialogue Editor | Alex Sawyer |
| Effects Editor | Julian Slater |
| Re-Recording Mixer | James Feltham |
| BBC Production Exec | Julie Scott |
| Sound Recordist | Dave Sansom |
| Make-up/Hair Designer | Jessica Taylor |
| Costume Designer | Emma Rosenthal |
| Script Editor | Elwen Rowlands |
| Casting Director | Andy Pryor |
| Production Designer | Brian Sykes |
| Music By | Edmund Butt |
| Editor | Sarah Brewerton |
| Director of Photography | Tim Palmer |
| Line Producer | Marcus Wilson |
| Exec Producers | Jane Featherstone |
| | Matthew Graham |

Viewing figures and audience data supplied by David Graham & Associates

# NORTH WEST DISTRICT C.I.D

Co-Created By
Matthew Graham
Tony Jordan
Ashley Pharoah

WRITTEN BY ASHLEY PHAROAH
PRODUCED BY CLAIRE PARKER
DIRECTED BY JOHN MCKAY

# CASE FILE

SERIES ONE
EPISODE FOUR

| | |
|---|---|
| DCI GENE HUNT | PHILIP GLENISTER |
| DI SAM TYLER | JOHN SIMM |
| DS RAY CARLING | DEAN ANDREWS |
| DC CHRIS SKELTON | MARSHALL LANCASTER |
| WPC ANNIE CARTWRIGHT | LIZ WHITE |
| WPC PHYLLIS DOBBS | NOREEN KERSHAW |

MUSIC

Brainstorm - Hawkwind
Jean Genie - David Bowie
Cross Eyed Mary - Jethro Tull
Silver Machine - Hawkwind
Gudbuy T'Jane - Slade
Wild Horses - The Rolling Stones
Blockbuster - Sweet
I don't Believe in If Anymore - Roger Whittaker

shooting script extract

**INT - SLAUGHTERHOUSE/FRIDGE - DAY 4/4 07.10**

The huge fridge is stacked with frozen cuts of meat. SAM and GENE are wearing thick coats, hats and gloves...GENE locks the fridge door and SAM and GENE stand with their backs against it. A beat.

                    GENE
          How did you know Red Rum was gonna win
          the National?
                    SAM
          Just a hunch.
                    GENE
                 (Suspicious)
          You didn't have inside information? A
          little bird in the racing fraternity?
                    SAM
          I wouldn't do a thing like that, would I?
                    GENE
          I didn't think you'd lock a murder
          suspect in a giant fridge.
                    SAM
          He didn't answer my question.
                    GENE
          I've a feeling he will.

EDWARDS'S fist start to thump against the doors, frantic.

                    SAM
          How's that animal in your stomach?

Gene looks down at his belly. Considers.
                    GENE
          I do believe he's sleeping.

Gene and Sam turn and open the doors...

# THE WARREN

## Drinks List

| | |
|---|---|
| Bitter | 20p |
| Lager | 19p |
| White Wine (Glass) | 14 |
| Red Wine (Glass) | 14 |
| Campari & Lemonade | 16 |
| ...no & Lemonade | 1 |
| | 1 |

**THE WARREN**

**VIP PASS**

Marc Bolan

The Warren, Manchester
Prop. Stephen Warren

Original Broadcast Stats
   Run Time: 58' 13"
   Transmission: Monday 30th January 2006,
                 9pm BBC ONE

Viewing Figures for original broadcast:
   Overnight:                        6.4 million
   Adjusted Ratings:                 6.6 million
   Audience Share:                   25.9%

        Adjusted figures include time-shift recordings.

There is a truce on the streets of Manchester between the police and local gangster Stephen Warren.

Gene believes that Warren can control the violence which is beyond the reach of the force and that ultimately it makes his patch a safer place to be. Sam has seen where this sort of police corruption will lead and believes no such thing...

There's no way he can take Warren on alone, however, and he begins to accept that he just may have to turn a blind eye.

Until he meets a young woman who is struggling to raise her four-year-old son on the limited money brought home by her fly-by-night husband. A woman who owes Warren rent on their small terrace...

A woman who happens to be Sam's mother...

NELSON — TONY MARSHALL
YOUNG GIRL — HOLLY-MAI LEIGHTON
EDWARDS — DAVID CORDEN
DRIVER — DENTON BROWN
→ MARC BOLAN — WILLIAM MATHESON
STEPHEN WARREN — TOM MANNION
JONI — KELLY WENHAM
ROYSTON — CHRIS WILCOX
MRS ( RUTH ) TYLER — JOANNE FROGGATT
CARROWAY — STEPHEN AINTREE

WILL ENJOY PRISON
(BUM BANDIT)

WHO?

Ruth Tyler
(AKA Joanne Froggatt)

Previous Form:
  The Street
  See No Evil: The Moors Murders
  Island at War
  Casualty
  A Touch of Frost
  Lorna Doone
  Coronation Street

| | |
|---|---|
| Stunt Co-ordinator | Ray L. Nicholas |
| Stunt Performer | Spencer Wilding |
| 1st Assistant Director | Joanna Crow |
| 2nd Assistant Director | Guy Barker |
| 3rd Assistant Director | Ellena Harris |
| Floor Runner | Thomas Alibone |
| Production Co-ordinator | Michael Noble |
| Assistant Co-ordinator | Tricia Carr |
| Production Office Runner | Lucy Patrick Ward |
| Continuity | Angie Pontefract |
| Production Accountant | Diane Pontefract |
| Assistant Accountant | Matthew Pope |
| Location Manager | Brett Wilson |
| Unit Manager | Joseph Cairns |
| Camera Operator | Nick Beek-Sanders |
| Focus Puller | Joe Blackwell |
| Clapper Loaders | Kim Tunstall |
| | Mark Dempsey |
| Grip | Ron Fleet |
| Sound Maintenance | Paul Watson |
| Gaffer | Brian Jones |
| Best Boy | Terry Eden |
| Electrician | Danny Griffiths |
| Genny Operator | Tony O'Brien |
| Art Director | Matthew Gant |
| Standby Art Director | Katy Tuxford |
| Art Dept Assistant | Nick Ainsworth |
| Production Buyer | Ian Tully |
| Props Master | Joe Malone |
| Dressing Props | John Fegan |
| | Neil Glynn |
| Standby Props | Neil O'Rourke |
| | Pete Moran |
| Standby Carpenter | Tom Higgins |
| Construction Manager | Hugo Slight |
| Police Advisor | Steve Crimmins |

| | |
|---|---|
| Costume Supervisor | Monica Aslanian |
| Costume Assistants | Becky Davies |
| | Joanne Evans |
| Make-up Supervisor | Juliet Jackson |
| Make-up Artist | Sarah Rahim |
| Casting Associate | Kirsty Robertson |
| Publicity | Premier PR |
| Post Prod Supervisor | Jessica Rundle |
| Post Prod Assistant | Anastasia Timeneys |
| Assistant Editor | Matt Cannings |
| Online Editor | Scott Hinchcliffe |
| Colourist | Jet Omoshebi |
| Music Advisors | Blind Beggar Ltd |
| Dialogue Editor | Alex Sawyer |
| Effects Editor | Julian Slater |
| Re-Recording Mixer | Nigel Heath |
| BBC Production Exec | Julie Scott |
| Sound Recordist | Dave Sansom |
| Make-up/Hair Designer | Jessica Taylor |
| Costume Designer | Emma Rosenthal |
| Script Editor | Elwen Rowlands |
| Casting Director | Andy Pryor |
| Production Designer | Brian Sykes |
| Music By | Edmund Butt |
| Editor | Sarah Brewerton |
| Director of Photography | Tim Palmer |
| Line Producer | Marcus Wilson |
| Exec Producers | Jane Featherstone |
| | Matthew Graham |

NOR~~TH~~
DIST~~~~

Co-Created By
Matthew Graham
Tony Jordan
Ashley Pharoah

SERIES ONE
EPISODE FIVE

# CASE FILE

WRITTEN BY TONY JORDAN
PRODUCED BY CLAIRE PARKER
DIRECTED BY SJ CLARKSON

| | |
|---|---|
| DCI GENE HUNT | PHILIP GLENISTER |
| DI SAM TYLER | JOHN SIMM |
| DS RAY CARLING | DEAN ANDREWS |
| DC CHRIS SKELTON | MARSHALL LANCASTER |
| WPC ANNIE CARTWRIGHT | LIZ WHITE |
| WPC PHYLLIS DOBBS | NOREEN KERSHAW |

When the dead body of a Manchester United Fan is discovered Gene is quick to lay the blame on a City supporter. With a derby match kicking off that weekend Sam is desperate to prove otherwise, only too aware of the riot they'll have on their hands should the crime be reported as football related.

His attempts to investigate are met with dismissal until he hits on the idea of going undercover amongst the United Supporters in the best place to keep an ear open — the local pub. Gene suddenly sees the benefits and joins Sam and Annie as Head Barman at the Trafford Arms for the night.

Chicken in a basket, anyone?

Some of the patrons, including Malcolm Cox and Pete Bond, are more outspoken in their desire for revenge. But was the murderer a City fan, as they believe?

ION ONE

**MANCHESTER U.**
**V**
**MANCHESTER CITY**
SATURDAY, APRIL 21ST
Kick off 3.00 p.m.

## Admission 35p

**PADDOCK**

UNITED ROAD

№ 733·243

№ 733·243

Issued subject to the Rules, Regulations and Bye-Laws of the Football Association. No Ticket exchanged nor money refunded.

**This Portion To Be Retained**

As a capacity attendance is expected, it is strongly recommended that patrons ENTER THE GROUND not less than 30 mibntes before kickoff

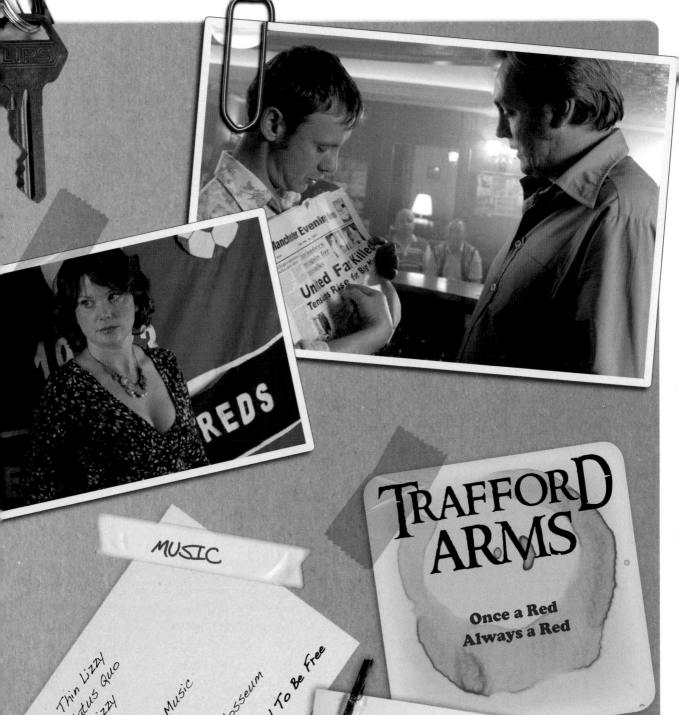

**MUSIC**

The Police – Thin Lizzy
Good Thinking – Status Quo
The Rocker – Thin Lizzy
White Room – Cream
Jeepster – T Rex
Would You Believe – Roxy Music
Urban Guerilla – Hawkwind
Ejection – Hawkwind
I Can't Live Without You – Colosseum
Mother Of Pearl – Roxy Music
I Wish I Knew How It Would Feel To Be Free – Nina Simone

**TRAFFORD ARMS**

Once a Red
Always a Red

Original Broadcast Stats
  Run Time: 58' 09"
  Transmission: Monday 6th February 2006,
        9pm BBC ONE
Viewing Figures for original broadcast:
  Overnight:
  Adjusted Ratings:                    6.7 million
  Audience Share:                      6.9 million
                                       26%

  Adjusted figures include time-shift recordings

| | |
|---|---|
| NELSON | TONY MARSHALL |
| RYAN | MICHAEL LAWRENCE |
| STANLEY COOPER | IAN BARRITT |
| PETE BOND | ANTHONY FLANAGAN |
| CRAIG | KRIS MOCHRIE |
| PAUL | STEVEN BLOWER |
| MAN IN PUB | JOHN WILSON |
| MALCOLM COX | JOE DUTTINE |
| UNITED SCUM | |

Pete Bond
(AKA Anthony Flanagan)

Previous Form:
Cracker
Shameless
Foyles War
All About George
State of Play

| | |
|---|---|
| Stunt Co-ordinator | Peter Brayham |
| Stunt Performers | Tom Aitkin |
| | David Anders |
| | Matt Da Silva |
| | Dean Forster |
| | Glen Forster |
| | Paul Howell |
| | Gary Kane |
| | Dominic Preece |
| 1st Assistant Director | Jonathan Leather |
| 2nd Assistant Director | Guy Barker |
| 3rd Assistant Director | Ellena Harris |
| Floor Runner | Thomas Alibone |
| Production Co-ordinator | Michael Noble |
| Assistant Co-ordinator | Tricia Carr |
| Production Office Runner | Lucy Patrick Ward |
| Continuity | Angie Pontefract |
| Assistant Continuity | Steve Walker |
| Production Accountant | Diane Pontefract |
| Assistant Accountant | Matthew Pope |
| Location Manager | Brett Wilson |
| Unit Manager | Joseph Cairns |
| Camera Operator | Nick Beek-Sanders |
| Focus Puller | Steve Smith |
| Clapper Loader | Kim Tunstall |
| Grip | Ron Fleet |
| Boom Operator | Ben Brookes |
| Gaffer | Brian Jones |
| Best Boy | Terry Eden |
| Electrician | Danny Griffiths |
| Genny Operator | Tony O'Brien |
| Art Director | Matthew Gant |
| Standby Art Director | Katy Tuxford |
| Art Dept Assistant | Nick Ainsworth |
| Production Buyer | Ian Tully |
| Props Master | Joe Malone |
| Dressing Props | John Fegan |
| | Neil Glynn |
| Standby Props | Peter O'Rourke |
| | Neil O'Rourke |
| Standby Carpenter | Tom Higgins |

| | |
|---|---|
| Construction Manager | Hugo Slight |
| Police Advisor | Steve Crimmins |
| Costume Supervisor | Monica Aslanian |
| Costume Assistants | Becky Davies |
| | Joanne Evans |
| Make-up Supervisor | Juliet Jackson |
| Make-up Artist | Sarah Rahim |
| Make-up Assistant | Adele Firth |
| Casting Associate | Andy Brierley |
| Publicity | Premier PR |
| Post Prod Supervisor | Jessica Rundle |
| Post Prod Assistant | Anastasia Timeneys |
| Assistant Editor | Matt Cannings |
| Online Editor | Scott Hinchcliffe |
| Colourist | Jet Omoshebi |
| Music Advisors | Blind Beggar Ltd |
| Dialogue Editor | Alex Sawyer |
| Effects Editor | Julian Slater |
| Re-Recording Mixer | James Feltham |
| BBC Production Exec | Julie Scott |
| Sound Recordist | Nick Steer |
| Make-up/Hair Designer | Jessica Taylor |
| Costume Designer | Emma Rosenthal |
| Script Editor | Elwen Rowlands |
| Casting Director | Andy Pryor |
| Production Designer | Brian Sykes |
| Music By | Edmund Butt |
| Editor | Colin Fair |
| Director of Photography | Balazs Bolygo |
| Line Producer | Marcus Wilson |
| Exec Producers | Jane Featherstone |
| | Matthew Graham |

WEST
T C.I.D.

Co-Created By
Matthew Graham
Tony Jordan
Ashley Pharoah

# CASE FILE

SERIES ONE
EPISODE SIX

WRITTEN BY
MATTHEW GRAHAM & ASHLEY PHAROAH
PRODUCED BY CLAIRE PARKER
DIRECTED BY JOHN ALEXANDER

| | |
|---|---|
| DCI GENE HUNT | PHILIP GLENISTER |
| DI SAM TYLER | JOHN SIMM |
| DS RAY CARLING | DEAN ANDREWS |
| DC CHRIS SKELTON | MARSHALL LANCASTER |
| WPC ANNIE CARTWRIGHT | LIZ WHITE |
| WPC PHYLLIS DOBBS | NOREEN KERSHAW |

Sam hears his mother's voice echo back from the future with alarming news: she's saying goodbye.

The doctors are turning off his life support machine at 2pm.

Terrified and desperate to prove he's still alive he struggles to think of a way of communicating with the present. Then a call comes through about a hostage situation at the Manchester Gazette, where three members of staff are being held at gunpoint. The armed man, Reg Cole, is proving very uncommunicative, even after Annie, Sam and Gene become further unwitting hostages.

He has made only one thing clear:

He intends to execute his prisoners at 2pm.

*shooting script extract*

INT. GAZETTE OFFICES - EDITOR'S SUITE
                    GENE
     Oh come on Reg, you're a criminal;
     you do what you do. I'm a copper; I
     do what I do. Cats eat kippers and
     dogs eat bones.

                    REG
     All I want is to tell the world what
     is in my head. And just for once to
     have them listen.
     I was going to release them. Then I
     would do what I had to do and the
     world would be left with my epitaph
     in the paper.

                    SAM
     Reg ...

                    REG
     But not now. You have dishonoured
     yourself and the price you pay is
     death. Two o'clock! On the dot!

Original Broadcast Stats
   Run Time: 58' 09"
   Transmission: Monday 13th February 2006,
                 9pm BBC ONE
Viewing Figures for original broadcast:
   Overnight:
   Adjusted Ratings:              6.2 million
   Audience Share:                6.6 million
                                  25%

   Adjusted figures include time-shift recordings.

# Manchester Gazette

## SIEGE ENDS PEACEFULLY AFTER GUNMAN STORMS OFFICES

# POLICE PRAISED IN HOSTAGE SWOOP

**EXCLUSIVE BY JACKIE QUEEN**

Earlier today DCI Gene Hunt and the officers of the North West District CID team took control of a hostage crisis at the offices of the Manchester Gazette. At approximately 8 o'clock this morning an armed man entered the building and took three hostages at gunpoint. Within the hour officers from CID arrived on the scene.

Officers of the Regional Crime Squad were also present both during and after the siege but left the resolution of the situation to the CID.

Editor-in-Chief Hugo Barton, his secretary Doris and reporter Jackie Queen were held, along with WPC Annie Cartwright who had courageously volunteered to go in under cover as a nurse. As part of the CID situation control procedure the hostages were later joined by DCI Gene Hunt and DI Sam Tyler.

The gunman, Mr Reginald Cole, had worked at the Gazette as a caretaker for many years and felt aggrieved that his services had never been properly recognised. This, together with personal issues dating back several years, had resulted in his protest which was intended to force the paper to print his story.

During the resolution of the crisis, DCI Hunt received a potentially fatal gunshot to his chest while risking his life to protect a member of the Regional Crime Squad who was standing in the line of fire.

'Luckily he had the foresight to be wearing protection' commented DC Chris Skelton of North West District CID.

Reginald Cole has been arrested and is expected to be charged with a number of offences relating to the siege and to the wounding

Inspector [...] Crime Squad [...] further stateme[...] the events, wh[...] view were b[...] investigation [...] findings will be [...] issue of the Ga[...]

DS Ray Carl[...] give us a brea[...] hostage proce[...] rigorously follow[...]

Involving [...] protection inc[...] to as the dou[...] controlled from [...] which was base[...] carpark for the [...]

NELSON — TONY MARSHALL
HUGO BARTON — CARL CIEKA
REG COLE — PAUL COPLEY
NERVOUS LADY — DEBBIE HOWARD
JACKIE QUEEN ← RUTH MILLAR
DORIS — MARGARET HENSHAW
GEORGE BATES — KEN DRURY
DCI LITTON — LEE ROSS

~~HACK JOURNO~~

BLOODY GOOD
REPORTER

Reg Cole
(AKA Paul Copley)

Previous Form:
The Street
Heartbeat
Shameless
Waking The Dead
Dead Man Weds
New Tricks
Born & Bred
Silent Witness
Peak Practice
This Life

| | |
|---|---|
| Stunt Co-ordinator | Ray L. Nicholas |
| 1st Assistant Director | Steve Robinson |
| 2nd Assistant Director | Guy Barker |
| 3rd Assistant Directors | Thomas Alibone |
| | Emily Williams |
| Production Co-ordinator | Michael Noble |
| Assistant Co-ordinator | Tricia Carr |
| Production Office Runner | Lucy Patrick Ward |
| Continuity | Angie Pontefract |
| Assistant Continuity | Steve Walker |
| Production Accountant | Diane Pontefract |
| Assistant Accountant | Matthew Pope |
| Location Managers | Brett Wilson |
| | Joseph Cairns |
| Camera Operator | Ken Lowe |
| Focus Pullers | Steve Smith |
| | Joe Blackwell |
| Clapper Loader | Kim Tunstall |
| Grip | Alex Coverley |
| Boom Operator | Ben Brookes |
| Gaffer | Brian Jones |
| Best Boy | Terry Eden |
| Electrician | Jimmy Bradshaw |
| Genny Operator | Tony O'Brien |
| Art Director | Matthew Gant |
| Standby Art Director | Katy Tuxford |
| Art Dept Assistant | Nick Ainsworth |
| Production Buyer | Ian Tully |
| Props Master | Joe Malone |
| Dressing Props | John Fegan |
| | Marcus Holt |
| Standby Props | Neil O'Rourke |
| | Pete Moran |
| Standby Carpenter | Tom Higgins |
| Construction Manager | Hugo Slight |
| Police Advisor | Steve Crimmins |
| Costume Supervisor | Monica Aslanian |
| Costume Assistants | Becky Davies |
| | Joanne Evans |

| | |
|---|---|
| Make-up Artists | Emma White |
| | Adele Firth |
| Casting Associate | Andy Brierley |
| Publicity | Premier PR |
| Post Prod Supervisor | Jessica Rundle |
| Prost Prod Assistant | Anastasia Timeneys |
| Assistant Editor | Matt Cannings |
| Online Editor | Scott Hinchcliffe |
| Colourist | Jet Omoshebi |
| Music Advisors | Blind Beggar Ltd. |
| Dialogue Editor | Alex Sawyer |
| Effects Editor | Darren Banks |
| Re-Recording Mixer | James Feltham |
| BBC Production Exec | Julie Scott |
| Sound Recordist | Nick Steer |
| Make-up/Hair Designer | Juliet Jackson |
| Costume Designer | Emma Rosenthal |
| Script Editor | Elwen Rowlands |
| Casting Director | Andy Pryor |
| Production Designer | Brian Sykes |
| Music By | Edmund Butt |
| Editor | Roy Sharman |
| Director of Photography | Grant Scott Cameron |
| Line Producer | Marcus Wilson |
| Exec Producers | Jane Featherstone |
| | Matthew Graham |

Viewing figures and audience data supplied by David Graham & Associates

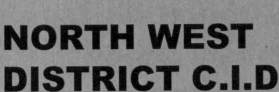

Co-Created By
Matthew Graham
Tony Jordan
Ashley Pharoah

# NORTH WEST DISTRICT C.I.D

WRITTEN BY CHRIS CHIBNALL
PRODUCED BY CLAIRE PARKER
DIRECTED BY SJ CLARKSON

# CASE FILE

SERIES ONE
EPISODE SEVEN

| DCI GENE HUNT | PHILIP GLENISTER |
| --- | --- |
| DI SAM TYLER | JOHN SIMM |
| DS RAY CARLING | DEAN ANDREWS |
| DC CHRIS SKELTON | MARSHALL LANCASTER |
| WPC ANNIE CARTWRIGHT | LIZ WHITE |
| WPC PHYLLIS DOBBS | NOREEN KERSHAW |

# NORTH WEST DISTRICT C.I.D

## OFFICER REPORT

Officer: DI Sam Tyler

Page 1 of 12

| Date: | Activity: |
|---|---|
| 0830 hrs | DS Carling, DCI Hunt ~~the university college~~ and WPC Cartwright ~~approximately 0837hrs~~ ~~chased the suspect~~ ~~chase and was arrest~~ ~~the custody cells at~~ |
| 0941 hrs | DCI Hunt, DS Carli~~Mr Billy Kemble, in t~~ but this was not p~~arrested the suspe~~ in powdered form. ~~manhandled the su~~ questioned furthe |
| 1005 hrs | DC Skelton and ~~some tea and co~~ ~~sandwiches.~~ |
| 1024 hrs | I assisted WP |
| 1245 hrs | carried out ro~~on current po~~ drugs use an |
| 1356 hrs | ~~suspect was~~ relating to c |
| 1500 hrs | Mr Kemble, |

# NORTH WEST DISTRICT C.I.

## OFFICER REPORT

Officer: DCI GENE HUNT

| Date: | Activity: |
|---|---|
| | NOTHING HAPPENED TODAY. |

Gene Hunt

Billy Kemble is a small-time drug dealer, a stepping stone to bigger and more important convictions, but when he dies in custody Sam begins to suspect a cover-up in the office.

Can he investigate his own colleagues? More to the point, can he afford not to?

With everyone against him and Gene trying to cover his officers' backs, Sam has some difficult decisions to make, and has to face the very real possibility that the bigger and more important conviction Billy Kemble could lead to will be an officer from CID itself.

Original Broadcast Stats
Run Time: 58' 03"
Transmission: Monday 20th February, 9pm BBC ONE

Viewing Figures for original broadcast:
Overnight:                62 million
Adjusted Ratings:         65 million
Audience Share:           24.6%

Adjusted figures include time-shift recordings.

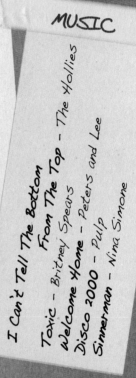

MUSIC

I Can't Tell The Bottom From The Top – The Hollies
Toxic – Britney Spears
Welcome Home – Peters and Lee
Disco 2000 – Pulp
Sinnerman – Nina Simone

*shooting script extract*

INT. ANDREA'S FLAT - DAY 7/2 14.31

GENE wanders around nosily. BILLY'S sister ANDREA is seated with SAM.

                    SAM
      The post mortem concluded that
      Billy died from a heart attack.
                  ANDREA
      Because of the fight he had.
                    GENE
      Afraid not, darling.
         (off a look from SAM)
      Seems a large quantity of cocaine
      skipped up his nose and conked out
      his heart.
                  ANDREA
      Drugs?

                    GENE
      Lot of dangerous hobbies, your
      Billy.

             SAM (gently)
      Did you know he used cocaine?
             ANDREA (adamant)
      He doesn't. He'd never take drugs.
                         (CONT.)

              it.)
                    GENE
      With respect, I'm sure you thought
      he kept his cock in his keks and
      all.
           ANDREA (to SAM re:GENE)
      Is he your boss?
             (SAM nods)
      What would I get for smacking him
      one?
                    SAM
      Round of applause from half our
      station.

NELSON          TONY MARSHALL
BILLY KEMBLE    KEVIN KNAPMAN
ALBERT COLLINS  ANDREW VINCENT
SAEED TAUFEEQ   SAGAR ARYA
DOCTOR          TOM LLOYD-ROBERTS
ANDREA KEMBLE   LISA MILLETT
SUPT. RATHBONE  WILLIAM HOYLAND
OSWALD SPEAR    NICHOLAS BLANE

Andrea Kemble
(AKA Lisa Millett)

Previous Form:
See No Evil: The Moors Murders
Vincent
No Angels
Blackpool
Clocking Off
Millions

| | |
|---|---|
| Stunt Co-ordinator | Peter Brayham |
| Stunt Performers | Gordon Seed |
| | Nick Wilkinson |
| 1st Assistant Director | Jonathan Leather |
| 2nd Assistant Director | Guy Barker |
| 3rd Assistant Director | Ellena Harris |
| Floor Runner | Thomas Alibone |
| Production Co-ordinator | Michael Noble |
| Assistant Co-ordinator | Tricia Carr |
| Production Office Runner | Lucy Patrick Ward |
| Continuity | Angie Pontefract |
| Assistant Continuity | Steve Walker |
| Production Accountant | Diane Pontefract |
| Assistant Accountant | Matthew Pope |
| Location Manager | Brett Wilson |
| Unit Manager | Joseph Cairns |
| Camera Operator | Nick Beek-Sanders |
| Focus Puller | Steve Smith |
| Clapper Loader | Kim Tunstall |
| Grip | Ron Fleet |
| Boom Operator | Ben Brookes |
| Gaffer | Brian Jones |
| Best Boy | Terry Eden |
| Electrician | Danny Griffiths |
| Genny Operator | Tony O'Brien |
| Art Director | Matthew Gant |
| Standby Art Director | Katy Tuxford |
| Art Dept Assistant | Nick Ainsworth |
| Production Buyer | Ian Tully |
| Props Master | Joe Malone |
| Dressing Props | John Fegan |
| | Neil Glynn |
| Standby Props | Neil O'Rourke |
| | Pete Moran |
| Standby Carpenter | Tom Higgins |
| Construction Manager | Hugo Slight |
| Police Advisor | Steve Crimmins |

| | |
|---|---|
| Costume Supervisor | Monica Aslanian |
| Costume Assistants | Becky Davies |
| | Joanne Evans |
| Make-up Supervisor | Juliet Jackson |
| Make-up Artist | Sarah Rahim |
| Make-up Assistant | Adele Firth |
| Casting Associate | Andy Brierly |
| Publicity | Premier PR |
| Post Prod Supervisor | Jessica Rundle |
| Post Prod Assistant | Anastasia Timeneys |
| Assistant Editor | Matt Cannings |
| Online Editor | Justin Eely |
| Colourist | Jet Omoshebi |
| Music Advisors | Blind Beggar Ltd |
| Dialogue Editor | Alex Sawyer |
| Effects Editor | Julian Slater |
| Re-Recording Mixer | James Feltham |
| BBC Production Exec | Julie Scott |
| Sound Recordist | Nick Steer |
| Make-up/Hair Designer | Jessica Taylor |
| Costume Designer | Emma Rosenthal |
| Script Editor | Elwen Rowlands |
| Casting Director | Andy Pryor |
| Production Designer | Brian Sykes |
| Music By | Edmund Butt |
| Editor | Colin Fair |
| Director of Photography | Balazs Bolygo |
| Line Producer | Marcus Wilson |
| Exec Producers | Jane Featherstone |
| | Matthew Graham |

# NORTH WE
# DISTRICT

Co-Created By
Matthew Graham
Tony Jordan
Ashley Pharoah

# CASE FILE

SERIES ONE
EPISODE EIGHT

WRITTEN BY MATTHEW GRAHAM
PRODUCED BY CLAIRE PARKER
DIRECTED BY JOHN ALEXANDER

| | |
|---|---|
| DCI GENE HUNT | PHILIP GLENISTER |
| DI SAM TYLER | JOHN SIMM |
| DS RAY CARLING | DEAN ANDREWS |
| DC CHRIS SKELTON | MARSHALL LANCASTER |
| WPC ANNIE CARTWRIGHT | LIZ WHITE |
| WPC PHYLLIS DOBBS | NOREEN KERSHAW |

Sam is becoming part of his new world, gaining in confidence and growing comfortable.

That's about to change.

A bookie's clerk is murdered and there's one suspect who Gene hopes will lead to them nailing the Morton brothers, a new crime syndicate in town.

Unfortunately for Sam, that suspect is Vic Tyler, his father.

Could this be the key to the visions he's been having since arriving in 1973? Could this be his way home?

MUSIC

Friday 13th – Atomic Rooster
The Rock – Atomic Rooster
Tokoloshe Man – John Kongos
In The Snow – Atomic Rooster
Devil's Answer – Atomic Rooster
See My Baby Jive – Wizzard
Life on Mars? – David Bowie
Meet Me On The Corner – Lindisfarne
Little Bit Of Love – Free

## Seized Films

Once Upon A Time In Her Vest

Fist Full Of Donnas

For A Few Donnas More

The Good, The Bad and The Humpy

The Wild Breast Bunch

The Man Who Shagged Liberty Valance

Riding Lonesome

Gang-Bang at the OK Corrall

The Maginificent Seven-In-A-Bed

Butch Cassidy and the Lapdance Kid

Destry Rides Again (And Again)

The Bumfighter

The Naked Spurs

Sexcoach

Way Out In Her Vest

Ride The High Country Women

*shooting script extract*

INT. POLICE STATION - LOST & FOUND - 12.05

VIC
Round and round she goes and where she stops .. is pretty obvious.
CHRIS taps the a card without the crease. VIC turns it over - Queen.

VIC
Lesson for me; never try to out-smart the copper's mind.

CHRIS
It's the investigative brain in't it. It's lava ... lava .. torial ..

SAM
Lateral. Lateral thinking Chris.
VIC smiles up at SAM and SAM almost faints.

VIC
Senior officer?

GENE (powers in)
Not that senior.

Original Broadcast Stats

Run Time: 58' 33"

Transmission: Monday 27th February 2006, 9pm BBC ONE

Viewing Figures for original broadcast:
Overnight:                    7.1 million
Adjusted Ratings:             7.4 million
Audience Share:               28.6%

*Adjusted figures include time-shift recordings.*

NELSON      TONY MARSHALL
VIC TYLER   LEE INGLEBY
RUTH TYLER  JOANNE FROGGATT
JIMMY LIPS  MATT CROSS
MANAGER     PAUL KEMP
YOUNG SAM   ALEXANDER O'LOUGHLIN

Vic Tyler
(AKA Lee Ingleby)

Previous Form:
The Street
Hustle
Early Doors
Clocking Off
Spaced

| | | | | |
|---|---|---|---|---|
| Stunt Co-ordinators | Peter Brayham | | | |
| | Tony Lucken | | | |
| Stunt Performers | Bruce Cain | | | |
| | George Cottle | Construction Manager | Hugo Slight | |
| | Dean Forster | Police Advisor | Steve Crimmins | |
| | Gordon Seed | Costume Supervisor | Monica Aslanian | |
| 1st Assistant Director | Steve Robinson | Costume Assistants | Becky Davies | |
| 2nd Assistant Director | Guy Barker | | Joanne Evans | |
| 3rd Assistant Director | Ellena Harris | Make-up Artists | Emma White | |
| Floor Runner | Thomas Alibone | | Adele Firth | |
| Production Co-ordinator | Michael Noble | Casting Associate | Andy Brierley | |
| Assistant Co-ordinator | Tricia Carr | Publicity | Premier PR | |
| Production Office Runner | Lucy Patrick Ward | Post Prod Supervisor | Jessica Rundle | |
| Continuity | Angie Pontefract | Post Prod Assistant | Anastasia Timeneys | |
| Assistant Continuity | Steve Walker | Assistant Editor | Matt Cannings | |
| Production Accountant | Diane Pontefract | Online Editor | Scott Hinchcliffe | |
| Assistant Accountant | Matthew Pope | Colourist | Jet Omoshebi | |
| Location Managers | Brett Wilson | Music Advisors | Blind Beggar Ltd. | |
| | Joseph Cairns | Dialogue Editor | Alex Sawyer | |
| Camera Operator | Nick Beek-Sanders | Effects Editor | Darren Banks | |
| Focus Puller | Steve Smith | Re-Recording Mixer | James Feltham | |
| Clapper Loader | Kim Tunstall | Asst Re-Recording Mixer | Oliver Brierley | |
| Grip | Ron Fleet | BBC Production Exec | Julie Scott | |
| Boom Operator | Ben Brookes | Sound Recordist | Nick Steer | |
| Gaffer | Brian Jones | Make-up/Hair Designers | Jessica Taylor | |
| Best Boy | Terry Eden | | Juliet Jackson | |
| Electrician | Jimmy Bradshaw | Costume Designer | Emma Rosenthal | |
| Genny Operator | Tony O'Brien | Script Editor | Elwen Rowlands | |
| Art Director | Matthew Gant | Casting Director | Andy Pryor | |
| Standby Art Director | Katy Tuxford | Production Designer | Brian Sykes | |
| Art Dept Assistant | Nick Ainsworth | Music By | Edmund Butt | |
| Production Buyer | Ian Tully | Editor | Roy Sharman | |
| Props Master | Joe Malone | Director of Photography | Grant Scott Cameron | |
| Dressing Props | John Fegan | Line Producer | Marcus Wilson | |
| | Neil Glynn | Exec Producers | Jane Featherstone | |
| Standby Props | Neil O'Rourke | | Matthew Graham | |
| | Pete Moran | | | |
| Standby Carpenter | Tom Higgins | | | |

# NORTH WEST DISTRICT C.I.D
# INTERNATIONAL RELEASE

Each episode for Life On Mars is cut in two different versions. One is cleared for UK television broadcast, the other is cleared for worldwide release and includes variations available on DVD and as broadcast on BBC America.

Track listings in the CID Case Files are for UK television transmission. The international soundtrack is as follows:

### Episode One
LIFE ON MARS? - DAVID BOWIE
BABA O'RILEY - THE WHO
WHITE ROOM - CREAM
FEEL TOO GOOD - THE MOVE
IF THERE IS SOMETHING - ROXY MUSIC
EASY LIVING - URIAH HEEP
LOOK AT YOURSELF - URIAH HEEP

### Episode Two
LIVE AND LET DIE - WINGS
SAGA OF THE AGEING ORPHAN - THIN LIZZY
ONE OF THESE DAYS - PINK FLOYD
DREAM LAND - THE UPSETTERS
YOU SHOULDN'T DO THAT - HAWKWIND
JUNGLE LION - THE UPSETTERS
JUNIORS WAILING - STATUS QUO

### Episode Four
BRAINSTORM - HAWKWIND
JEAN GENIE - DAVID BOWIE
CROSS EYED MARY - JETHRO TULL
SILVER MACHINE - HAWKWIND
GUDBUY T'JANE - SLADE
BLOCKBUSTER - SWEET
I CAN'T CHANGE IT - FRANKIE MILLER

Episodes Three, Five, Six, Seven & Eight remain as detailed in the case files.

# A Look at the Series Pitch

## The Series

From the makers of *Spooks* and *Hustle* comes a brand-new drama series. Exciting, compelling, intelligent and highly original, **Life On Mars** is a cop show. With a twist.

DI Sam Williams is a true 21st Century hero. Passionate, thoughtful, committed almost to the point of obsession in his pursuit of justice (think Guy Pearce in *LA Confidential*). Sam does things by the book because he believes that the system evolved for a reason. But he is about to have his ordered world blown apart.

Because a few minutes into the show, our hero, Sam Williams, crashes his jeep in his local East London neighbourhood. And wakes up...in 1973.

Is Sam in a coma? Has he gone back in time? The audience may never know the answer, but the question will send shivers down their spines (and will no doubt become a source of fevered debate on the net...)

Initially disbelieving, Sam is forced to accept that he is living in the '70s, where Stratford Police station are expecting him to start work. Almost immediately, Sam is thrown into life as a cop in 1970s London. From this point on, the series is packed full of high-octane police investigations. Each episode is based around stories which will twist and surprise at every turn.

Like the best cop shows, **Life On Mars** is incredibly taut and dramatic throughout. But this series has an additional tension which arises from its unique premise. By taking a character so completely of our times and throwing him head first into our recent past, we are creating an opportunity to explore what makes us what we are today – and have some fun along the way.

Every idea starts somewhere...and before a project even gets as far as a script commission, most require a slick pitch document to encapsulate the idea for the potential broadcaster. The pitch needs to convey confidence in the idea and should be clear...

...and well-defined. Here's a few exclusive extracts from the original Life On Mars pitch. Some of the ideas fell by the wayside but many of the predictions came scarily true ('fevered debate on the internet', anyone?)...

# kudos

## LIFE ON MARS

An 8 x 60 minute returnable series

Created by

Matthew Graham
Tony Jordan
Ashley Pharoah

**SERIES OUTLINE**

April 2004

## Sam Williams (early 30s)

At the heart of every story is a conflict: Sam's belief that his knowledge of the future gives him superiority and a more evolved sense of policing. He is shocked and repulsed by his colleagues' attitudes to crime-solving. They conduct searches without warrants, threaten violence to get confessions, are racist and sexist, not just to the public but to each other.

But Sam quickly discovers that without 21st Century technology at his finger-tips, crime-solving in the 1970s relies on a more grass-roots approach, which means relying more on instinct – a quality Sam had previously considered himself to have a flair for. But what shocks him even more is that sometimes, contrary to what he has always believed, conducting an investigation without the usual lawyers, psychiatrists, social workers and warrants actually gets to the crux of a crime faster – and sometimes in a way that is more beneficial to everyone, including the suspects. In short, although he is loathe to admit it, Sam has as much to learn from the 1970s as they have to learn from him.

Although the last thing most of his colleagues would admit to is learning anything from their new (and strange) colleague. Least of all Sam's superior, Gene.

## Gene Burrows (early 40s)

A huge brute of a man, Gene Burrows would seem to be 1970s policing personified: arrogant, sexist, insensitive, slobbish, boozy, impatient, corrupt. He's everything that Sam has grown up believing is at the root of the problem for the police. And Sam is expected to work for him. BUT Gene has the command of his officers, he is forceful in his pursuit of criminals. And he gets results. Although they are at opposite ends of the spectrum when Sam first arrives, over the course of the series, the two actually start to forge a new dimension in their relationship. Not mates exactly. But not enemies either. A classic buddy partnership is formed.

From the original draft of the script, the leading character had gone through lots of name changes, From Tom Page through to Sam Tyler. At this point Sam's surname was Williams. Others up for consideration included Jackson, Hunt, Blair, Pointer and Heath...

...Gene's surname for most of the development was Burrows.

Sam's eventual surname choice was a result of Matthew Graham asking his daughter for suggestions – 'Tyler' was her choice.

## Sam's Journey

Alongside the main crime stories of the week, we also follow Sam's personal quest as he asks why and how he has entered this strange world.

What would you do if you could go back to your childhood – as an adult? What unanswered questions would you seek to find out? Who would you want to see again?

Sam quickly realises that 1973 is the year his dad left the family home. And the last time Sam saw him. He is suddenly presented with a unique opportunity: he can seek his dad out and persuade him not to leave. But did things turn out like they did for a reason? What happens if you change your own history?

Which is where Annie comes in.

## Annie (late 20s)

The chemistry between WPC Annie Cartwright and Sam is electrifying from the moment they meet. Unlike their other unreconstructed colleagues at the station, Annie is prepared to listen to Sam's apparently crazy concerns about having fallen back in time. As the series progresses, she comes to tolerate and even take small steps of faith towards believing Sam. But she is also a voice of reason to remind him that even if he *has* returned to his past, things happened the way they did for a reason. Perhaps he should leave things as they were...

Throughout the series, the motor that keeps pushing Sam on is his desire to find his father, resolve his past and get back home. But the trouble is that the longer Sam stays in this world, the harder he's finding it to remember what "home" is. And whether he wants to leave everything he's found here to return there...

The audience will be desperate to tune in each week to see whether Sam and Annie can admit their feelings for each other, despite the barriers of time.

Matthew Graham's wife gave birth to their son in 1999 shortly after Life On Mars was first developed. Is it an uncanny coincidence that their son is also called Sam?

Annie started life as Dr Michelle Standing, a Geordie medical school trained doctor, who - in the first draft of the original 1998 script - is fascinated by the fact that Sam isn't quite like the other guys at the station...

## Tone

The series will work on many levels. First and foremost, it is pure entertainment. Great stories filled with sexy, electric characters and a powerful love story at its heart.

Alongside the energy of the drama, the setting of the seventies will inevitably allow for a lightness of touch. Everyone will be able to enjoy the clothes, the over-sized hi-fis, the out of date cars, the lack of technical equipment. But these will always be played for real, part of the context of the series and never a distraction from the drama at its core.

Like Sam, we will rack our brains to see if we could remember the outcome of any sporting events of the '70s that we would be able to bet on. Or laugh when Sam tries to write a hit novel called *Jaws*. If only he could get past "The shark was huge and always hungry…"

But crucially, this is also a series that reflects effortlessly on society today. So when we follow a story about football hooliganism in the 1970s, like Sam, the audience will initially feel relief that those dark violent days have gone. But then, through Sam, we rediscover the joys of football untainted by corporate sterility. And, in another episode, we see how the glamorisation of the police force in the 1970s, which seemed so harmless at the time, was, in effect, the beginnings of the public mistrust in the police, which we all suffer from today.

## The writing and creative team

**Life on Mars** is created by the writers behind hit BBC1 series *Hustle*: Matthew Graham *(POW)*, Tony Jordan *(EastEnders)* and Ashley Pharoah *(Paradise Heights)*. Individually they all have impeccable TV pedigrees, but the force of their combined creative collaboration is exciting and unique. For **Life On Mars**, they have worked together to create stories, characters and a premise that will hopefully challenge and satisfy audiences everywhere.

The series will be produced by BAFTA, EMMY and RTS award-winners Kudos, makers of *Hustle*, *Spooks* (BBC1) and *Psychos* (C4).

**Lee Thompson** would like to say big thanks to:

All at Kudos, including Claire Parker and Rebecca Ferguson for all their help.

Matthew, Tony and Ashley who created a show that so many love.

John, Phil, Liz, Marshall, Dean, Noreen and Tony, for bringing the characters to screen.

Claire Potter for all her support, and for believing in us.

Cameron Roach, Marcus Wilson, Sam & the girls at the production office for helping us in Manchester.

Nicki 'Burning Bright' Ballantyne, for her effervescent energy and making us feel welcome on set.

Matt Gant for his time, help and multitude of production photos.

Mark 'Vimto' Ashmore for making me chuckle, and for looking cool in a hi-vis jacket.

Steve and Ian, for their patience and understanding.

To Lee Binding, for inspiration, and a good many laughs.

All the guys at The Railway Arms (www.railwayarms.com) for their support and kind words.

Those behind The Annotated Martian (www.versaphile.com/lom/) for an invaluable resource.

And finally praise be to Sally, whose keen eye stopped us from making fools of ourselves.


**Guy Adams** would like to say:

Well now … it's difficult isn't it when one's colleague does as good a job of thanking all the relevant people as you can see above? Allow me to take this opportunity to say: yes! He's quite right, they were all lovely and I'd happily live with the lot of them in one big squat.

So, to move on to the more personal thanks: most particularly Bruve, Seph and 'Nuls for putting up with my uselessness as we tried to sell a house, a business, pack up all our combined belongings and run off to live in another country. You may have had to do most of the packing love, but at least I know who was the second assistant director on episode seven … ahem … sorry.

Also, I'm told by my mother that I've never dedicated a book to her which makes me somewhat of an ungrateful little swine when you consider how many of my other family and friends have been dropped into some narrative or other along the line. So, let it be known that I hereby show my immense love and consideration to Diana Adams by promising to dedicate the next book to her.

This one goes out to that bloke I met down the supermarket this morning … the one with the silly left ear. Hope you like it.

Pocket Books, Guy Adams and Lee Thompson would like to thank the following for providing photographs and for permission to reproduce copyright material. While every effort has been made to trace and acknowledge all copyright holders, we would like to apologise should there have been any errors or omissions.

Life on Mars? © 1971 David Bowie
Lyrics reproduced by kind permission of Tintoretto Music / RZO Music Ltd / EMI Music Publishing Ltd / Chrysalis Music Ltd

Except where noted here, all images © Kudos Film and Television.
Photographs on page 7, 46, 54, 58, 67 & 128 were supplied by Lee Thompson.
Photographs on page 35 (Empty Test Card), 48, 50, 51, 52, 53, 55,108 & 153 (Gene Newspaper Portrait) were supplied by Matt Gant.
Rafaella Hutchinson portrait (page 35) supplied by Tim Palmer.
Post Production images (pages 71 & 73) supplied by Matt Wood of 3sixtymedia.

Train Carriage photo (page 10) © Jeroen Belen
Brighton Pier photo (page 27) © Simon Stratford
Big Ben photo (page 27) © Anka Draganski
Bristol Canal photo (page 27) © Dog Madic

'Buster' comic © Egmont Fleetway / IPC Magazines Ltd. All Rights Reserved.

David Bowie photo (page 65) © Debbie Doss/Contributor/Hulton Archive/Getty Images